Healed by Animals

Stormie Conway

Livonia, Michigan

The events described in this book are true. However, some names, locations, and breeds of dogs have been changed to protect those who prefer their identities to remain anonymous.

Editor: Hannah Ryder

STORMIE'S HEART
Copyright © 2020 Stormie Conway

All rights reserved. No part of this publication may be reproduced, distributed, or transmitted in any form or by any means, including photocopying, recording, or other electronic or mechanical methods, without the prior written permission of the publisher, except in the case of brief quotations embodied in critical reviews and certain other noncommercial uses permitted by copyright law. For permission requests, please write to the publisher.

Published by BHC Press

Library of Congress Control Number: 2020934350
ISBN Numbers:
978-1-64397-142-1 (Hardcover)
978-1-64397-143-8 (Softcover)
978-1-64397-144-5 (Ebook)

For information, write:
BHC Press
885 Penniman #5505
Plymouth, MI 48170

Visit the publisher:
www.bhcpress.com

For Tony Abbate, Steve Frysinger, and Gina Bores.
Love you, my friends.

Acknowledgments

Dedicated to the glory of God who, in His grace, endowed me with the ability to express my thoughts in writing. And to all my clients who entrust their beloved pets to my care and, by extension, provide me with enough material to fill a book.

"Life's an open-house party. Bubbles, squirrels, a dried leaf skittering across the road…invite them all."

~ Duncan ~

Stormie's Heart

One

Rory, a black cocker spaniel, and Mr. Fantl, Rory's pale, almost translucent human—a pair of old souls who provided my first foray into pet care.

When I was in sixth grade, a friend and neighbor mentioned that the elderly and disabled man who lived next door to us on the corner needed someone to walk and feed his dog. Freddy had been caring for Rory, but tired of it and told me the job was simple and straightforward. Mr. Fantl lived alone in the big house, and would pay $25.00 a week (a fortune for a twelve-year old) to someone who would walk Rory up the street and back before and after school, and brown some hamburger meat for Rory's dinner. The work would require no more than half an hour a day.

I visited with Mr. Fantl whom I'd never met, and found him to be a soft-spoken man who loved his dog, and wanted nothing more than for Rory to be comfortable. I agreed to walk and feed Rory, beginning the next day, and the routine was just as Freddy had described.

The most difficult part of the job was hearing Mr. Fantl moan and cry out in agony as he soaked his feet that were covered with terrible gangrenous sores in some solution. I can hear his wails still, sometimes incoherent, sometimes calling for his Rory.

Soon after I'd begun caring for Rory, I saw a sky-blue mohair sweater in the window of a local clothing store. Mohair sweaters were all the rage back then and a luxury I could only dream of having. Despite growing up in a house where both my parents worked—my father during the day, and my mother at night—money was never available for nice clothes or good food. Cigarettes, alcohol, and junk food took too large a bite out of take-home pay. Makes me wonder how I grew up as healthy as I did—a nonsmoker, nonalcoholic, and a conscientious food shopper.

One evening, I mentioned the mohair sweater to Mr. Fantl. He wrote a check to me without hesitation for the cost of the pretty thing.

I don't remember how long I continued to care for Rory or if I found another person to replace me when I stopped. But as I reflect back on my time with Mr. Fantl, I wish that I'd possessed then some of the genuine understanding and compassion for others, especially for our elderly population, that we seem to acquire only as we age and experience sadness and tragedy for ourselves.

Two

Fast forward to when I was eighteen years old in the late sixties and living in the first digs that I could call my own, meaning that I had my own space separate and apart from my parents' house. It wasn't much—just a large single room with a small kitchen and bathroom, and located on the ground floor facing a noisy busy street. But I thought I was so cool in my independence with my two-seater chartreuse Fiat convertible, my good-looking nice-guy boyfriend, my stereo and lots of future-classic-rock records, a secretarial job in a small office…and a too-cute-to-be-legal German Shepherd mix puppy that I'd rescued from some shelter. In my mind, I had it all!

One afternoon, I tried my hand at painting the joint living room/bedroom, and managed to get what seemed like an equal amount of blue paint on the floor and myself as on the walls. Some also dripped onto the tips of Nadia's ears while she sat nearby watching me with a critical eye. In vain, I tried to wash the oil-based paint off her with soap and water. A cloth moistened with turpentine removed most of the paint from her ears. But Nadia cried within seconds of the oil making contact with her skin.

I took her to a vet as soon as I located one who could see her right away, and who told me in disgusted tones after hearing my story, "You don't deserve to own a dog." I'll never forget those words. He washed the remaining paint from her ears using some non-irritating solution, and soothed Nadia's pain. I left the vet's office feeling an uncomfortable mixture of relief and shame.

Nadia was a phenomenal little dog whom I could trust to follow me from the apartment building's adjacent parking lot to my front door without a leash. That is, until one gut-wrenching afternoon during rush hour when time slowed to a crawl and then jerked to a halt. The traffic light about a hundred feet away turned green, the drivers of the stopped cars gunned their engines and sped toward my puppy, who for whatever reason, chose that moment on that day to run into the middle of the street. I watched in transfixed horror as the first car hit Nadia, ran her over. And I watched the car that killed her not even slow down. Nobody stopped.

In hysterics I ran to my upstairs neighbors and friends, Judi and Aron. Aron went outside to check on Nadia, but returned several minutes later shaking his head. I don't remember seeing her mashed body in the street when I returned to my apartment later. Maybe Aron removed her when he was outside. If so, I shall always be grateful.

Three

I owned a beautiful adult German Shepherd for a short time. My younger sister first told me about the dog, saying that the person who owned him couldn't keep him, and was looking for a good home for him. After promising Kathy that I would never abandon the dog, she talked to her friend who gave the dog to me. I fell in love with Izek the instant I saw him, and brought him home with me.

Home for me by this time was a large room and a private bath that I rented in a big old Victorian-style house owned by a divorced man with two Siamese cats. I hadn't asked Mr. Kidder beforehand if I could bring a dog home with me, but when he saw Izek, he agreed to let me keep him so long as I kept him in my room. Done.

While I worked during the day, I tethered Izek outside with a long rope to the side of the house with a bowl of water and shelter under the steps from inclement weather. I cringe when I think about treating any dog like that now, but I was young at the time—early twenties, maybe late teens. I didn't know or didn't think about how a large dog needed room to run. All I cared about was that I loved him, and that was enough. Maybe it was enough for Izek, too. Dogs ask little in return for the gift of their hearts. Today, I would never confine a large dog to a single room, and I would never tether a dog of any size for an extended period of time.

I walked Izek everyday as soon as I returned home from work, and drove him to the park on weekends. Must have been a sight with this large dog sitting in the passenger seat of my two-seater Fiat, a car not much larger than one of those chariots that shuttles folks through some amusement park rides. Please keep paws inside the cart until it comes to a complete stop.

For all my unintentional mistreatment of him, Izek knew I was his human. Even when I left the door to my room open when Mr. Kidder wasn't home, Izek remained with me. He never ventured into the hallway, let alone down the stairs, until…

Mr. Kidder was a quiet man, and he led a quiet life. He did, however, belong to a local theater group. One night when he returned home after a performance, and I hadn't heard the front door open, Izek sprang from where he'd been lying in my room and ran down the stairs. Before I could go after the dog to see what had alerted him, I heard Mr. Kidder call my name. *Uh-oh!*

I will never forget the frozen-in-time tableau that met my eyes when I reached the top of the stairs and looked down at the entrance hall. Izek stood on his hind legs with his front paws against Mr. Kidder's shoulders pinning him to the inside of the front door. Mr. Kidder and his two guests looked terrified. Although Izek showed no signs of aggression and released his "prisoner" as soon as I called him, I can imagine how frightening it must have been for Mr. Kidder to see a full-grown German Shepherd hurtling down the stairs toward him. And then to have the dog "capture" him. Clearly, Izek was protecting me and maybe the house, too, and this had to be a good thing. Yes? I prayed that Mr. Kidder would begin to appreciate the dog rather than just tolerate him.

But this was not to be the case. The following day, Mr. Kidder told me that his cats were upset by the presence of the dog to the point that they no longer left the bedroom to sit with him in the living room during the evenings while he read or watched television. Izek would have to go.

I was distraught. What to do with him? I wouldn't put him in a shelter. Neither my conscience nor my stomach would allow me to abandon him to the streets. I didn't know anyone who wanted a dog, let alone an adult German Shepherd, no matter how well-trained or sweet-tempered. And I didn't want to move back into my parents' house again, assuming that were even a possibility.

The only solution my young ignorant brain could come up with was to have Izek put to sleep. I had never put an animal down, and I didn't know where to begin or whom to call or where to go. Beside myself with despair, I called Norman Walz, a pastor and friend, for guidance. I knew Mr. Walz through his son, John, who performed in the same theater group as Mr. Kidder. Mr. Walz volunteered to accompany me to a vet, and assured me that euthanizing an animal was a simple, quick, and painless procedure. The animal received a shot, went to sleep, and was gone in a heartbeat. It did not suffer at all.

Despite the comforting words of Mr. Walz, I broke into uncontrollable tears the moment I walked Izek into the vet's office. When asked by the receptionist what was wrong with the dog, I answered through sobs, "Nothing. I can't keep him. I have to have him put to sleep." "Wait here," she said, and walked away from her desk. The receptionist returned a few minutes later and told me she'd spoken to someone who had acres of property, a farm in fact, and this man would adopt Izek if that was okay with me. Blessed relief such as I'd never felt flooded through me.

I hugged the receptionist, and left with Mr. Walz for the address in Randolph that we'd been given. When we pulled into the driveway, I saw several people working outside on a barn. Most of them stopped what they were doing, walked toward us, and reached down to greet Izek as I led him over to them. I knew in an instant that I'd made the right decision in bringing the dog to the farm. He'd found a perfect forever home with lots of space and people around him. My broken heart began to mend.

Four

Renters of the second upstairs bedroom in Mr. Kidder's house came and went during the eighteen months I lived there. One young couple, after hearing soft mewling coming from the basement, investigated the source and discovered a stray cat. A stray cat who was a new mom!

While Rob and Lorraine acted like adults and discussed with Mr. Kidder the broken window through which the cat most probably had gotten into the house, I followed my emotions and beat it down to the basement to see the babies. So tiny! The kittens' eyes had yet to open. I ran back upstairs to fill a bowl with milk for momma and returned to the basement where I indulged my inner child and did what came naturally to me: I picked the kittens up one by one and cuddled the precious bundles.

A few days later, my ankles and lower legs started to itch. I mean itch to the point that I scratched them until they bled. No ominous red rash indicating I'd come into contact with poison ivy. And to the best of my knowledge, no allergy to cats. But copious amounts of calamine lotion, witch hazel, and other tried-and-true remedies failed to provide so much as a modicum of relief.

For two days, I went to work with my ankles wrapped in gauze bandages, and sat at my desk with my feet soaking in a shallow pan of cool water all day. How wretched must I have felt to sacrifice my dignity, and to endure the not-so-subtle stares and smirks from colleagues.

Enough! I went to a doctor who, figuring my itchiness had to be allergy related, prescribed a kind of spray cortisone with instructions to spray the affected area something like every eight hours. I went through the entire can in two days. Such was the extent of my misery and the ineffectiveness of the prescribed medicine to relieve it.

Then, one evening at dinner, Rob mentioned that he'd been experiencing similar symptoms, although not as severe as mine. He hadn't felt compelled to wrap his ankles or carry a pan to work in which to soak his feet. Lorraine remained asymptomatic, as did Mr. Kidder.

Later the same night while I soaked in the bathtub as opposed to standing under a shower, I saw a small black fleck floating in the water. A flea! *Gross!* All became clear in an instant. I thought back to the many times I'd gone down to the basement to feed Mama Cat and cuddle the kittens. The fleas must have jumped onto me and then onto Rob, maybe after having first landed on the carpet upstairs. For whatever reason, Lorraine and Mr. Kidder escaped the sadistic mini fiends.

I scrubbed my skin and scalp raw after discovering the source of my torment. A phone call to Animal Control, and our kitty squatters were taken into custody for a flea bath and fostering. An insecticide treatment of the basement, and a thorough vacuuming of all carpets ensured the fleas, too, were no more. And I experienced immediate and sublime relief from nonstop itching.

But I gained a firsthand perspective of what dogs and cats endure when infested with fleas, and I wouldn't wish such torture on anyone or anything. It's said that God created everything with a purpose in mind. Well, it appears from my limited experience that He alone can claim cognizance of a flea's purpose.

Five

The next memory of my younger years is of Christmas at the home of my dear friends, Mary and "Snurf" (the latter so named because of a typo he'd once made). Family and friends gathered around the dining room table for the holiday dinner, plates laden with good fixin's that had been served buffet style in the kitchen. Animated chatter and laughter over the clink of silverware filled the room.

Then a solid thump from the kitchen. Silence and startled expressions replaced the smiles and conversation that had held sway moments earlier. Snurf, seated nearest the kitchen got up to see what had happened. His laughter broke the tension and brought us all up from the table and into the kitchen.

Their small cat, Meowie Cat, had crept into the kitchen lured by the aromas of delicious people food, and unable to resist the temptation, had jumped onto the table and begun to help herself to the glazed ham. In her enthusiasm, she managed to drag the entire ham, almost as big as she was, onto the floor.

Not sure if it was the danger of the boulder-size ham she saw falling on her or the sound of it hitting the floor that unnerved Meowie Cat and sent her scuttling for safety, but by the time we'd all gotten to the kitchen, she had slunk halfway back to her prize with pieces of telltale ham still hanging from her mouth. Her eyes and body language reflected her acute craving for a second go at the meat, and the promise of more mischief to come if not thwarted by meddling humans. Any sign of guilt or repentance for her thievery of Christmas dinner leftovers was nowhere evident in the little girl's demeanor. Instead, a resolute mini-cougar awaited her chance to return to her "kill."

Cell phones hadn't come into existence yet, so she wasn't caught on camera burglarizing the kitchen. It occurred to me that a video "sent to Sagat" of Meowie Cat making off with the Christmas ham might have yielded a small financial windfall for Mary and Snurf. And maybe because we'd piled our plates with plenty before Meowie Cat helped herself to the considerable spoils, we found the entire incident just too funny to be angry.

But I think Snurf may have closed Meowie Cat in a separate room after the incident…and on future holidays when the unattended kitchen table sagged with good eats.

Six

Over the years, several friends have entrusted me with riding their horses whenever I've wanted and without supervision, a privilege for which I've tried to prove myself worthy—except for one time when I allowed pride and poor judgment to override any sense of integrity. The fallout was immediate, and my loss exorbitant.

Buttercup belonged to a friend with whom I worked at Bell Labs before I'd bought Flame, my Arabian gelding. I'd had a few riding lessons here and there, and Sue knew me to be a less-than-expert rider. But after seeing me ride Butter a few times, she gave me permission to ride her in the ring and paddock outside the barn where she boarded the horse. One caveat: Butter loved to jump. Keep her away from all cross rails and other jumping obstacles for her safety, as well as my own. I promised to do so.

I rode Butter every chance I got after work and on weekends when Sue wasn't planning to be at the barn. I sat to the trot, changed leads at the canter, and tried to post; success of the latter would not be attained for several years.

Then one Saturday morning while riding Butter, arrogance consumed me. I made the deliberate decision to ignore Sue's instructions and took Butter over a cross rail in the ring. And then I took her over another one. And then I looked up and saw Sue walking across the field toward me.

Shame washed over me. As I dismounted Butter and led her to the fence, the hurt in Sue's eyes devastated me. And when she reached for the reins and said, "Let me have my horse," my heart sank as the magnitude of my selfishness registered off the charts. I tried to apologize, but my words sounded hollow even to me. There was nothing I could say or do to compensate for how I'd betrayed Sue's trust in me. Sometime later, I learned that Butter had turned up lame a few days before I'd jumped her, and the vet had advised that Butter be exercised at nothing harder than a trot. When Sue saw Butter jump, she not only saw a disregard for her instructions, but she watched her baby being ridden harder than she should have been.

That Saturday morning, I lost more than the joy of riding Butter; I lost a good friend. Sue's attitude toward me in the workplace remained one of consummate professionalism. She neither condemned me nor treated me with disrespect or unkindness.

But thirty years later, she and I reconnected through the miracle of Facebook when I sought her blessing to include this story in my book. Sue's lack of hesitation in allowing me to recount the incident, and her suggestion that we reunite over breakfast in a local diner assuaged three decades of guilt. How sweet forgiveness! Since that wonderful breakfast during which it seemed the bad stuff never happened, Sue and I have hooked up a few times. I consider it one of God's many gifts to us that chance opportunities present themselves for friends to get together after decades of separation, and pick up where they left off without missing a beat.

In retrospect, I don't think I could have handled someone, a supposed friend, with the same degree of class as Sue showed me after my betrayal. A lesson in grace to be sure—one that I hope to remember and practice should I ever find myself in a similar situation with the roles reversed.

Buttercup

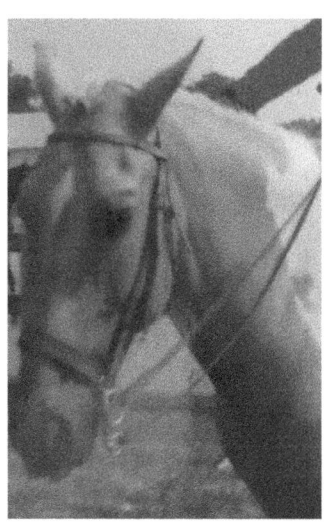

Seven

"It followed me." All the times I used that line as a child when I tried to explain each enticed-to-come-home-with-me mutt to my parents, and they never bought it—not once. Didn't matter how adorable, how young or old, how sweet the puppy or dog that had "followed" me home happened to be. My parents always tracked down the animal's rightful owner or called animal control, or just closed the door and let it find its own way to from wherever it had come. But for lots of short whiles, I got to pretend that I had a dog of my own.

I'm older now—much older—and haven't lost the urge to bring home all things cute and fuzzy.

Case in point: One evening, after having exercised Flame (my horse of yesteryear) and cleaned his stall, I pulled out of the driveway of the farm where I boarded him and saw in the glare of my headlights a yellow Lab standing in the road. I stopped the car, approached the dog, and saw that he wore no collar. So of course I did the only thing any self-respecting dog lover and dog-owner wannabe would do. I encouraged him into the hatch of my Volkswagen Rabbit and drove him home to where Steve waited for me.

Steve, an environmental scientist with a bunch of letters after his name, indulged and supported most of my eccentricities. And true to form, after having welcomed the dog into the house, he made a run to the store for all necessary dog paraphernalia while I remained at home getting to know our new friend.

We named the dog Spice because of his cinnamon-colored fur, and by next morning Spice had wormed his way deep into our hearts. Neither Steve nor I failed to notice how well-cared for and how well-behaved Spice seemed for a stray, and after talking it out, we agreed to notify the police of the dog's whereabouts. It was the right thing to do. Some heartbroken family probably wondered what had happened to their pet, but Steve and I made no secret of hoping that Spice would remain unclaimed for a full week—the unwritten length of elapsed time before we could assume that no one would contest our ownership of the dog.

Some days passed before we noticed that Spice showed little interest in textbook behavior for Labs—that of chasing and retrieving balls and sticks. And then one morning while talking to Spice about the day ahead, I saw the characteristic milky cloudiness of cataracts forming in his eyes. A local veterinarian referred me to a veterinary ophthalmologist who had removed cataracts from the eyes of some dogs. Despite having had Spice for less than a week, I wanted to give him the chance to see. To that end, I packed him up in my Rabbit, and away we went on the two-hour drive to Lawrenceville. But the trip turned out to be for naught as the doctor advised me that Spice was too old (much to my surprise, given his level of apparent health), and the cataracts too well-developed to risk surgery. It broke my heart to hear this prognosis, and I returned home feeling disappointed and sad.

One week to the day after I'd brought Spice home, Steve came home from work with devastating news. A woman had called him that afternoon saying she'd spoken to the police about her missing dog, an old yellow Lab. The police had given her Steve's office number, and Steve, after speaking with the woman, knew her to be the rightful owner of Spice. She would come to our house later in the evening to collect her dog.

Steve and I braced ourselves when we saw the high-end sedan pull into our driveway, and forced welcoming smiles on our faces when we answered the doorbell. I don't remember the woman's name, but I sensed a kindness and warmth about her. When she saw the dog and called, "Morgan!," it was clear that our "Spice" belonged to her. They loved each other, and the woman bubbled with gratitude over how well Steve and I had cared for her Morgan. I think she felt sorry in one sense about taking Morgan from us, and she went to considerable lengths to assure us that he would return to a caring home. She shared stories about Morgan's puppyhood, and how he grew up in a family that loved him to pieces. They, too, were aware of the cataracts and had researched the possibility of having them removed. Before she left us, the woman gave me a scarf she'd bought while in Europe as a thank you to us for loving Morgan.

After she and Morgan were gone, Steve and I held each other and cried.

A fundamental belief of the Christian faith centers around the assurance that when God closes one door, He opens another. While I had waited to see the canine ophthalmologist, I saw a woman with a long slinky weasel-like creature on her arm. I asked her what it was, and she told me it was a ferret. I'd never heard of ferrets before, but I fell in love with the animal (that cute-and-fuzzy thing again) and knew right then that I wanted one. Steve expressed reservations about the acquisition of such a critter, and I would have to wait a few years until our relationship changed and I moved into my own apartment before I would own the first two of fifteen ferrets.

Eight

Soon after Steve and I parted ways in September or October of 1984, my emotional state shattered and descended into what doctors diagnosed as clinical depression—a disinterest in life, a sense of despair, and a well-developed suicidal ideology. My sudden uncontrollable crying jag one day at AT&T stunned and upset my coworkers, and prompted me to call my friend, Eddie, who worked as a Mental Health Associate at Fair Oaks, a local private psychiatric hospital.

Eddie's eyes and spirit evoked the kind of trust the young have in Santa Claus, and the old would have if they believed in him. I'd known Eddie for years through our mutual friends, Mary and Snurf, and had spent countless hours huddled with him over the kitchen table, always accompanied by some delicious confection, discussing life's dragons and how to vanquish them. In truth, I would have trusted Eddie with my life.

After the near-hysterical phone call to him from AT&T during which I attempted to explain what was happening in my head, and in response to my questions and fears about whether I should sign into Fair Oaks, he asked me with all the kindness in the world (and I remember his exact words), "Would I work in a place that hurt people?" Decision made.

Steve drove me to Fair Oaks later that night. Crying again in the admissions office, I asked the person behind the desk if I'd be home in three weeks for Thanksgiving. "There's a good chance." I felt heartened by those noncommittal words, and was escorted onto the Evaluation Unit from where I heard the heavy magnetized steel doors slam with finality behind me, and from where I turned and watched through the narrow pane of reinforced glass as Steve walked away.

The days and weeks passed. Steve came to visit me at least once a week, much to the chagrin of the hospital staff, who felt Steve's presence was a deterrent to my getting well. (They later admitted to being wrong about Steve when they realized his and my relationship was one that would change—not terminate—as time passed.)

I made friends with some of the patients on my treatment unit, and felt safe and happy enough to the point that I no longer wanted to be discharged. Thanksgiving came and went. Christmas came, and I spent my holiday pass with John—my knight in shining armor who had once protected me from an army of rampaging grasshoppers—and his family. A wonderful Christmas, indeed, as I shared the spirit of the season with three generations of John's warm, loving, and close-knit family, including his dad who had accompanied me to the vet with Izek several years before.

One day in the hospital, I was upset over something that had happened and mentioned my feelings to the substitute psycho-dramatist before our group session. He responded with something to the effect that if time allowed, he'd get to me. For forty-nine of the fifty minutes, I stewed and got angrier with each passing moment while the group, guided by the facilitator, focused on another patient. With less than a minute remaining, the therapist addressed me and asked me what was going on. I spilled my guts, after which he said, "Well, time's up for today." He then herded our group out the door and back to the main unit, leaving me hanging—raw and livid.

When we returned to the unit, I paced like a tiger in a cage with mounting distress and rage. Motion and sound from other patients assaulted my frayed nerves. I went to the nurse's desk and asked for permission to go to the "quiet room," because I felt like I was spiraling out of control.

Once inside the small windowless room, noise level on the unit lowered by several decibels, and all other stimuli vanished. A mental health associate observed me through a camera and saw me begin to cry and claw at my arms in agitation. She came inside with me and offered a thick telephone book for me to shred as a safe means to vent whatever demons seethed inside me. I attacked the book with a vengeance.

Sometime later, the creative therapist for my group entered the quiet room where I sat exhausted on the floor with my back against the wall and strips of telephone book scattered around me. She sat on the floor with me and told me she had a live bunny in the therapy room. Would I come to session? I wouldn't have to participate in any artsy craftsy kind of thing. I could just hold the bunny. How brilliant! This woman knew how to reach me. The simple thought of the chance to love a bunny calmed me and ignited my desire to rejoin the other patients. I accompanied her to session and sat on a chair in a corner with the therapy bunny on my lap while the other patients busied themselves with painting, embroidering, or assembling small mosaic knickknacks. A few people interrupted their work to walk over to me and ask if they could pet the bunny before returning to their projects. Of course.

I've always believed in the healing powers of animals. Therapy dogs—angels on four legs—possess legendary abilities to raise the spirits of the depressed, sick, and injured. After my experience with the bunny, I'm convinced that four-legged angels also come in the form of bunnies, as well as horses, cats, ferrets, and any other of God's esteemed creatures. An intangible purging catharsis happens when an animal submits itself to comforting a hurting person without questions, without agenda, and without judgment.

Nine

Some years after I'd sold Flame, a friend granted me access to her horse, a spirited palomino trained in barrel racing, but quiet and steady on trails.

One day as Goldie and I exited the woods onto the narrow path skirting the far side of the large riding ring, Goldie punched her stampede button. I received no heads-up signal from her, and no outside stimulus that I could see triggered her flight. She was walking, and then she was running. I'd never experienced so sudden a transition in a horse's pace, and I think to this day that it was a miracle I wasn't thrown backward from the saddle. I mean I was super relaxed as always after a ride through the trees, the reins held loosely in my hands, my mind drifting through hazy daydreams as I rocked in the saddle to Goldie's easy gait. Had I not been taken by complete surprise and scared out of my wits, I think I would have enjoyed her smooth and fast gallop. Instead, I was terrified. But in the midst of this heart-stopping high, my brain somehow continued to work. My first thought: I can't turn this horse around in a tight circle to slow her down. Woods on one side of us and the corral's fence on the other left no room for such a maneuver. My second thought: If I fall off, I'll be killed.

After the longest minute or two, Goldie slowed to a walk on her own, and I thought I'd regained control. Not so. Within a few strides—just long enough for me to almost catch my breath—she plunged forward and resumed her hell-bent mission to wherever or whatever she had in mind. Around the far turn and heading for home. My third thought: This is embarrassing. I hope no one sees me.

Goldie, upon approaching the barn door, slowed to a walk and stopped on command. I dismounted and almost crumpled to the ground on legs without working knee hinges. Goldie allowed me to lead her inside while looking for all the world like the most angelic of beasts. Without much of a stretch, I could imagine the glow of a halo she made visible to anyone who saw her.

It wasn't until I'd fastened her with cross ties in the barn aisle that I noticed my bleeding hands from where the leather reins had sliced through my fingers when Goldie first sprang from some dreamed-up starting gate that she alone could see.

A grateful nod to Julie, my riding instructor at Snowbird so long ago, for instilling me with confidence in my seat without the use of hands…and for teaching me the technique of turning a runaway horse in small tight circles to regain control. Even though I couldn't employ that maneuver, it prevented my mind from shutting down in panic while riding out Goldie's junket.

Ten

I fancy myself an animal rights activist despite never having attended a PETA protest or any other such media-grabbing event. But a rebellious streak in me, perhaps a remnant from the sixties, fantasizes about participating in some radical exploit like releasing laboratory animals from their cages or picketing small fairs where elephants stand shackled in leg irons.

In my heart of hearts, I believe the continued abuse of animals in so many venues—circuses, rodeos, bull fights, laboratories—all in the names of entertainment and medicine is nothing short of shameful. These practices warrant damnation or at least outlaw status. I, however, aside from voicing my contempt around the water cooler of those who would abuse animals, or writing the occasional incensed letter to local newspapers, have done little to further this cause that I support with every fiber of my being. And my inaction leaves me with no choice other than to hang my head and categorize myself as a closet activist.

But one day while working at AT&T years ago, I saw my chance to make a tangible but not insignificant difference.

Vendors visited the complex every day during lunch hour. They'd set up their booths above the main cafeteria and sell everything from trinkets to housewares to clothes to fine jewelry. You name it, and a vendor sold it in our hallowed halls.

One afternoon, fur coats and jackets hung in profusion on racks. Fur mittens, scarves and earmuffs covered tables. Not faux furs—the real bloody deal—fox, raccoon, rabbit, mink, and other such creatures that had been raised for no other reason than to be slaughtered for their fur. I'd never seen a furrier at AT&T, but a conspicuous sign hung near his display that promised this particular furrier would return the following week. I felt sick.

Having lost my appetite, I returned to my desk and stewed until lightning struck. I drew up a petition with signature lines protesting the presence of the furrier. Pelts from once-living animals were not something we employees wanted to see while eating. We didn't support the killing of animals for their fur. Stylish faux fur having the look and feel of real fur could be found in the fanciest boutiques. Corduroy was invented so animals could keep their fur. Animals needed their fur more than we did. In short, do not allow the vendor to return next week.

A couple of coworkers, Lisa and Ashe, sharing the same heart and mind as I regarding the wearing of fur, helped make copies of the petition and distribute them. When lunch hour was over, we returned to the cafeteria and placed several copies of the petition on each table, upper and lower levels, for people to read and sign the following day. We also placed copies in all the men's and ladies' bathrooms, and on the windshields of cars in the underground garage.

I never learned how many signatures were collected, but the furrier did not return the following week. So while I never spray-painted the windows of a furrier or took an active part in any kind of illegal demonstration, I feel that Lisa, Ashe, and I made an important difference in the fight against raising animals for their fur. And I feel good about it still and so appreciate the support of my two partners in crime.

Eleven

As you might expect, I abhor the practice of poaching, and it breaks my heart to hear stories of animals being killed, with or without permits for no reason more noble than to indulge the selfish whims of some humans. The following is a Letter to the Editor I wrote and submitted to some local newspapers:

Two friends hunch over a chess board while one player ponders whether to move his knight or pawn. By chance or choice, the players think not of the sights and sounds over the African savannah where an agonizing scene unfolds, one that reveals the brutal and bloody origins of the cherished ivory chess pieces: the throbbing engines of low-flying helicopters that carry poachers commissioned to obtain the tusks from which game pieces will be carved, the gut-wrenching sight of panicked elephants stampeding across the plain from the helicopters; the staccato bursts of rifle fire felling the helpless animals; or the scream of chainsaws cutting savagely through tusks. The chess players don't imagine the bloodied savannah strewn with these magnificent largest-of-all land mammals lying slaughtered for no other reason than to sate narcissistic humans' craving for ivory…and the money to be made by satisfying this craving.

The demand for ivory exists in almost every country of the world, and the unscrupulous supply the market without hesitation and regardless of means. In 2013 alone, 20,000-plus African elephants were killed for their tusks. Much talk these days centers around preserving the earth for our grandchildren. What quality of planet do those who encourage poaching envision? One of nothing more than rock and steel? Clearly, it doesn't matter to some hypocrites preaching "save-the-planet" slogans that future generations will never see those species of awesome animals unfortunate enough to possess some characteristic, however small, that humans list among their must-haves.

Ivory. The word for some conjures images of elegant refinement and gentility. A pair of earrings hacked by a chainsaw from a slaughtered elephant's bloodied mouth. How distingué! "The earth lies defiled under its inhabitants." Isa. 24:5 (NIV)

Twelve

One afternoon while driving on the back roads home from work, I saw what appeared to be a dead adult raccoon. I slowed the car to get a closer look. Had it still been alive, I would have either stopped and attempted to retrieve it so I could take it to a vet, or I would have backed up and run over it to kill it and end its suffering. It was dead.

A little further up, a man stood by the side of the road with four little creatures crawling at his feet. He must have noticed that I slowed for the raccoon, because he flagged me down. I saw that the animals wriggling around were baby raccoons. Their mama had to have been the raccoon I'd passed.

I got out of the car to look at the kits who were so small that I could hold each of them in the palm of my hand. I don't think their eyes were open yet, but their lungs were well-developed. The little animals screeched nonstop.

The man told me about a rescue center somewhere over by the Great Swamp, a protected marshy area deserving of its name about half an hour away, and asked if I would take them. When I told him I would be happy to do so, he gave me the telephone number of the rescue facility, and a box in which to contain the raccoons. Their cries in the enclosed car as I continued home just about drove me nuts.

When I arrived home to the apartment complex in which I then lived, I called the rescue center and described what had happened. I told the woman who answered the phone that I couldn't deliver the raccoons until after midnight when my boyfriend got off from work. Would that be okay?

"Sure, bring them over then."

I called Vinny, whom I'd known only a year or so at the time, and asked him to stop by my apartment as he sometimes did after he got off work. But I didn't tell him about the raccoons, or that we'd have to transport them to the rescue center when he arrived.

During the five or six hours before Vinny arrived, I offered the babies a milk-soaked cloth on which they could suck to get something into their bellies. Soon after, the kits went to sleep in their box. Sublime silence.

Shortly before Vinny was due to arrive, I put the box containing the raccoons in my car and waited outside for him. As soon as he pulled into the parking lot, I ran over to him and with little explanation, instructed him to get in my car. I handed the box containing the awake and squealing babies to him, jumped behind the wheel, and tore out of the lot.

All sorts of credit to Vinny the Wookiee (so named with affection after the furry "Star Wars" character) who with good reason was annoyed, but allowed himself to be railroaded into a madcap late-night flight for the sake of four infant raccoons. I was tired and half-crazed enough to stop at a red light just long enough to make sure no traffic was in sight, and then proceed straight through it despite the police station located near the corner. Didn't do much to improve Vinny's frame of mind.

We careened over unlit roads through wooded Jockey Hollow Park on our way to the Great Swamp. The closed-in car, the darkness, and the late hour all combined to amplify the raccoons' screaming, which drove Vinny and me to near distraction.

We reached the sparsely populated streets of the Great Swamp and located the shelter, a private house. I don't remember much about the place, other than we entered through the kitchen where I saw several cages containing a menagerie of critters in various stages of rehabilitation. Despite my unnerved state of mind after our desperate passage through the night, I admired the shelter's dedication in providing for sick and injured animals.

And I am forever grateful to Vinny for his willingness to forgive and forget, or maybe overlook the intensity with which I react to an animal or animals in crisis.

Thirteen

Before I moved into a cottage in Chester around 1997, the previous tenant advised me that a herd of whitetail deer visited the stand of woods maybe a hundred feet from the house and waited for her to feed them. Maureen implored me to continue feeding them. They depended upon her, she said. And they were semi-tame, unafraid of her. No twisting of my arm necessary to comply with her request. In fact, I couldn't wait to see all the deer and make friends with them.

To those ends, I bought and maintained a supply of fifty-pound sacks of corn outside my back door. Got pretty good at slinging the sacks over my shoulder and carrying them from my car down the uneven fieldstone path without assistance to the covered bin beside my patio. Felt like Farmer Stormie. And then, twice a day—before I left for work in the morning, and late afternoon when I returned home—I'd scoop corn into a bucket and walk out to where the deer waited for me. They remained where they stood as I walked among them doling out the corn in long rows. Sometimes they began eating before I'd emptied the bucket. But I never could entice them to come within two feet of me and eat from my hand. *Sigh!*

During the seven years I lived in the cottage, I observed some amazing natural dynamics between the deer. Most people think of deer as timid docile creatures. Not so when among their own kind, and depending upon the season. Turns out that when the bucks' antlers are covered with velvet, the does do not allow bucks to eat with them. They kick them and chase them away. But when the antlers lose their velvet signaling that bucks have begun their rut, the tables turn one hundred and eighty degrees. The bucks feed, and the does wait from a distance until the bucks have eaten their fill. On rare occasions, a doe might approach one of the bucks and reach up to touch her nose to his in an act of submission. If the buck responds without aggression, the doe can begin to eat. But more often than not, the buck will chase the doe away.

The same kind of submissive/aggressive behavior occurs when the does show up with their babies during the spring. So long as the fawns remain close to their respective mothers, the herd with few exceptions will allow them to eat. But a rebellious or adventurous fawn that wanders away from its mother has a hard time returning to the fold. It, too, must then "beg" for food as the does did with the bucks the previous fall by touching its nose to that of an adult.

Early one Saturday morning while dew glistened on the grass, I glanced out the kitchen window and saw the tiniest fawn wobbling around on its spindly legs. I walked through the cottage and checked all the windows for sight of its mother. I looked into the woods, across the fields, and into the wine berry patch, but I did not see the doe.

Knowing that the fawn could not survive on its own if its mother had been injured or killed, I thought to corral the baby and take it somewhere safe like the Popcorn Zoo, a reputable wildlife refuge in South Jersey. The deer would have a good chance of making it to adulthood if protected at that facility.

~ Stormie's Heart ~

So I went outside to recheck for the mother. No sign of the doe. I rounded the side of the cottage just in time to see the fawn run behind the house. When I walked around back to where I'd seen the baby disappear, I saw no sign of the fawn. Where could it have gone? Only acres of fields lay beyond the cottage.

I turned and began to retrace my steps, and then saw the fawn's muzzle—only the muzzle—poking out from the pachysandra patch that hugged the cottage. But of course. The baby's instincts had led it to find a place to hide. How tiny must it have been to conceal itself within a ground covering such as pachysandra! And I still saw no sign of its mother as I looked again toward the woods and wine berry patch that bordered the fields nearest the cottage.

I approached the fawn one slow step at a time. The little creature remained frozen in place as I walked toward it, bent down, picked it up, and cradled it in my arms while thinking I would put it in my car and take it to the police station for direction.

I enjoyed one split second of inner fuzziness reveling in the opportunity I'd been given to save this beautiful wild thing from certain death if left on its own. But the instant I picked the fawn up, it issued forth with a single bellow that would rival that of a full-grown angry bull. It seemed impossible that such a terrible sound could come from such a small creature. Its bawl sliced through the silence of the morning with such force that, as I learned later, my neighbor heard it from inside his house fifty yards away.

At the sound of the fawn's cry, I saw its mother's head appear above the wine berry bushes. I carried the baby to within ten feet of the doe, set it down, and backed away. As the fawn approached its mother, I had concerns that the doe would reject her fawn. To my immense relief, I saw no such signs of rejection.

But a few hours later, I saw that same fawn teetering about by the side of the cottage again. Just a rebel, I concluded, that might one day assume the role of alpha buck in a herd. I have since learned that does leave their babies, sometimes for hours, and often in close proximity to humans where predators fear to approach and attack it.

∼

Another encounter with a baby deer. While driving through the woods on my way to work at AT&T, I saw a fawn—larger than the one that had hidden in the pachysandra—lying in the grass by the side of the road. It appeared unhurt as it rested on its elbows. It also appeared to be very much alone.

I stopped the car and got out for a closer look. When I walked over to the deer, it didn't flinch. I saw no sign of injury, but felt uncomfortable leaving it there on the forty-mile-per hour curvy road while people rushed to get to work.

I, despite having no clue as to what to do with the fawn, made the deliberate choice to stand vigil over the animal until some kind of help arrived. If I showed up late at the office, so be it. My priorities were clear and not open for debate.

After some time had passed, I watched a large truck approach, slow, and come to a stop a few feet beyond from where I stood. A robust, almost stereotypic-looking truck driver stepped down from the cab and made his way over to me. He looked at the fawn for a bit and expressed a depth of compassion for the animal that I found incongruous with the man's size and appearance. And then he asked if I'd mind if he brought the deer with him to the Popcorn Zoo, which he'd be in the vicinity of later in the day. I thought this a great idea and watched the man take the fawn (that remained silent, unlike the rascal that had lurched about in my backyard) in his arms and clasp it against his broad chest before walking back to his truck, and placing it in the cab. When I could no longer see the truck's tail lights, I returned to my car and marveled at the gentleness of the brawny truck driver who took the time to stop and volunteer to transport a vulnerable baby animal to a safe haven where it could mature and be returned to the wild.

Fourteen

Twenty-something years ago, while I lived in Chester, a dear friend adopted a cat that had been hanging around her niece's house during the winter. Lilly, as the cat came to be called, was on the small side but felt chubby when Alice picked her up. A few weeks after having taken Lilly in, Alice heard weak mewing from under her bed. Lilly had given birth to a black kitten. Two smaller kittens followed. Obvious deformities were apparent in the legs of the latter two babies, while the first kitten's front legs appeared short but well-formed.

Days passed, and Alice fretted about what to do about the kittens. In response to her concern, I suggested she take them to a veterinarian for evaluation. She did so, and as I recall, was advised to have them put down. Reluctant to have them destroyed, she told me she wanted to get a second opinion.

I referred Alice to my own vet and volunteered to accompany her, Lilly, and the three kittens after she'd made the appointment. We both anticipated a difficult time with the vet. Two of the kittens could barely walk because of their deformities, and although neither of us voiced the obvious, I think we both believed that they should be put out of their misery.

The vet concluded that Mama Lilly had contracted some sort of virus while pregnant, which had caused the deformities. When the vet examined the two kittens with the most severe deformities, she was shocked to discover in one kitten that the veins, rather than running the length of the leg, encircled the tibia and fibula. The other kitten's veins, while not perfect, were nowhere near as bad, although one hind foot faced skyward. The third kitten with the shortened legs appeared otherwise normal.

Alice decided to keep this last kitten, and a technician agreed to take the one with the turned-up paw. But the third little one—there was no way, in good conscience, Alice could ignore its condition. The kitten could not manage one step on its mangled legs. Alice looked at me for confirmation, and I nodded my head.

The process of euthanizing an animal is a simple one. Sedate them and then inject the drug to stop the heart. Easy on the animal and comforting to the owner in its painlessness and speed.

Not so for our kitten with the twisted veins. Try as she might, the vet found no vein into which she could inject a sedative. Alice couldn't look, but I watched with morbid fascination as the vet was left with no choice but to sedate the kitten with an injection into its neck. Alice's heart shattered, and I was happy to have been there for her. I feel like I'm the recipient of support so much more often than I provide it.

Mama Lilly's health deteriorated, and Alice had to have her put down as well. But JoJo, he with the short legs, thrived for many years. He and Alice lived at the end of a country road that bore almost no traffic, and where he enjoyed being outdoors on warm sunny days, and being indoors with Alice when the weather turned cold or rainy.

In 2006, JoJo disappeared for several days. Because JoJo was a tomcat, Alice was not too concerned until she next saw him in a neighbor's yard crying. He would not come to her as he always did, so Alice went to him and saw with stomach-turning horror that he was infested with botflies. She drove him to an emergency vet in Newton where they kept him overnight. Alice brought JoJo home the next day and noticed that, during the next several days, he always tried to get outside. Perhaps to go somewhere and die? Then early one Sunday morning, he entered Alice's bedroom frothing at the mouth, seeming anxious, and appearing to have difficulty breathing. Within a minute, he collapsed on the floor and took his last breath. Friends and neighbors stopped by to support Alice and help her bury JoJo in the backyard. Alice admits she still has difficulty remembering his last days, but takes comfort in knowing that she gave her JoJo a good life, and that he loved her so much that he came to be with her at the end.

Since that sad time, Alice has adopted Sweetpea. An adult when Alice took her in, Sweetpea is now a healthy twelve-year-old, indoor-only cat.

Fifteen

I had worked until 11:00 the previous night. Next morning at 5:00, a Saturday, I returned to the office. MCI filed lawsuit after lawsuit against AT&T during the nineties and had done so yet again. Overtime pay for those of us in the Law Department who wanted it was ours for the asking.

The sun just cleared the horizon as I drove the back roads to the office. Horse paddocks lined both sides of the road, and I allowed the early morning pastoral scene to calm my still-frazzled mind from the previous fifteen-hour working day. I forced myself to take deliberate long slow breaths and had attained a level of peace when a rabbit ran out from the bushes smack dab in front of my car.

In a single instant, dread rocketed through my senses and wiped out any semblance of the inner peace I'd worked so hard to attain. I slammed on the brakes, swerved away from the rabbit, but could not avoid hitting it. Already in tears, I got out of the car and saw that the rabbit was badly hurt, bleeding, and worst of all, still alive. In near hysterics, I wrapped the rabbit in a towel from my car, performed an illegal Uturn, and drove up to Vinny's house.

Though not living with Vinny at the time, I had a key to his house. I let myself in and walked into the dark bedroom where Vinny still slept. I stood there crying while holding the animal in a bloody towel until Vinny woke up. In retrospect, I can only imagine the shock he felt upon opening his eyes from sleep and seeing a person, even a person he knew, standing next to his bed crying and holding a bloody towel and a half-dead animal in her arms. I must have looked like something out of a horror movie. Stephen King's *Carrie* comes to mind.

But Vinny somehow kept his cool. He took the rabbit from me and carried it out to the kitchen while I remained in the bedroom. When he returned (without the rabbit), he insisted it was dead. "No, it couldn't be," I insisted. "Its heart was still beating. I could feel it." Vinny assured me the heart had indeed stopped, and what I had felt in the rabbit was a kind of postmortem spasm. He then dressed and took the rabbit down to Hopatcong State Park about a mile away. "No one will bother it there. I'll put it in a quiet place behind some bushes."

I accepted Vinny's explanation with some reluctance until I could convince myself that it made sense. And for my own peace of mind, and to minimize the chance of nightmares into the indefinite future, I agreed to his plan for laying the rabbit to rest.

For weeks, maybe months afterward, I obsessed about that rabbit whenever I got behind the wheel of my car. A friend advised me that if I continued to concentrate on the incident, I would draw a similar incident into my life. She told me she always visualized her car and tires, as well as rabbits and squirrels, surrounded by white light before she drove anywhere. A kind of positive energy inhaled from the universe. I took up the same practice. It calmed me. The last thing I wanted to do was think a second rabbit into the road in front of my car.

While I don't bother with the "white light" deal much anymore, I still sometimes invoke its power when I'm driving at night through wooded areas or if I sense mystic vibes of foreboding spawning within me.

Sixteen

After leaving AT&T in 1995, I obtained my paralegal certificate while working for a large prestigious law firm. I then left my full-time word processing position with the firm in search of paralegal work—even temporary work—and collected unemployment during those times when paralegal/legal assistant work was unavailable. A rocky few years for me indeed.

Vinny retired in 2000, and a few years later I moved in with him. I'd been having a difficult time making ends meet in my apartment, and it was too hard for Vinny to subsidize me without his AT&T paycheck.

A fall down a flight of stairs in 2009 resulted in serious injuries to my face and one of my legs, and while recuperating, I made the decision to never work a regular job again. Vinny's generosity in allowing me to stay with him provided the direct catalyst for the genesis and continuation of my pet-sitting business, as well as the indirect opportunity for the writing of this and my previous book.

Our next-door neighbor, Rose, to whom I'd spoken maybe once or twice—enough to ascertain our mutual love for animals—phoned me one day to tell me she'd found an injured bird, and to ask for ideas about where she might take it for medical help. I suggested the Raptor Trust, a fabulous facility located in the Great Swamp about forty-five minutes away that specialized in the treatment and rehabilitation of injured birds.

And then I didn't see or hear from Rose again until one afternoon at least a year later when I recognized her at a neighborhood barbecue to which we'd both been invited. Our friendship then took root.

Turkish-born and a recent U.S. citizen, Rose could never find it in her heart to turn any dog or cat in need away. (Unlike me who asked people not to tell me about abandoned ferrets. I would take them all if I could, but it would be neither practical, nor fair to Vinny. I knew ferrets existed out there in dire need of a good home, but I couldn't save them all. Had adopted one that a friend of a friend no longer wanted. Sushi was thin and sick when I brought her home and, within a month, I had to have her put down. Never again.) As a result of Rose's inability to refuse aid to animals, she worked like a fiend caring for two dogs, as many as nine cats at times, and two bunnies—in addition to her husband Andy, and her young daughter Z, also an animal lover.

Rose's modest house was given over to her critters. The dogs lived downstairs in a separate room, complete with two sofas and a doggie bed and plenty of food and water. And the cats were separated according to how they got along with each other. Result: three floors with cats, at least three litter boxes, and at least three food and water bowls.

Oh, and a bunny (sometimes two bunnies) lived in a hutch in the garage. When weather permitted, they moved to their "summer hutch" outdoors during the day.

Rose and her family moved to Connecticut a few years ago, but before they relocated, I had the opportunity to care for her petting zoo numerous times. And while doing so, I learned that the laws of physics must have ceased to exist in Rose's world. How else could she have found the time and energy to care for all her critters (including taking them to the vet as needed), taxi Z to dance classes, gymnastics, and play dates, prepare meals, and maintain a clean house? All this in addition to always being there for anyone in the neighborhood who needed a helping hand. On several occasions when Vinny and I went away for a weekend or longer, Rose and Z would stop by our house twice a day, every day, to feed my ferrets, clean their cage, and let them out to play.

In return for her assistance with the ferrets (for which she never accepted a dime in return), I offered a deep discount when caring for her menagerie. And hers was the only assignment for which I never packed a suitcase. Just walked next door four times a day with a list of what I needed to do. I tried early on to employ the time management training and organization skills I'd acquired at AT&T, but either I'd forgotten the techniques or I'd never mastered them at all. While not a difficult gig, it constituted a real project with the sheer number of animals, and dispersed as they were throughout the house.

The early morning visit around 6:30 was the trickiest, further compounded most times by my being not quite awake. All the animals needed to be fed. The dogs had to be walked. Bunny wanted his cage cleaned. And three, maybe four litter boxes needed to be cleaned. Lots of food dishes and water bowls to check and fill. After much trial and error and a lot of wasted time, I managed to massage all the tasks into a reasonable facsimile of an ordered routine.

The rabbit presented the single toughest challenge. Because the cage was tricky to open and close, I didn't clean it every day. I hated leaving it uncleaned for even one day, let alone three, but I was more afraid that the bunny might escape and be impossible to catch. Or worse, find itself in the clutches of one of the many cats.

My final-day-of-any-assignment routine includes emptying all waste baskets, taking the garbage out to the trash can, making certain that all animals have fresh water and a clean cage, stall, or bed, and returning the house to the shape it was in before the owners return home—a plan, I'm told, that never fails to please. But the universe sometimes plays a game of fifty-two pickup with me, a contest that I almost always lose. Prime example: the assignment in which Andy, slated to return late in the afternoon a day or two before Rose and Z, arrived home twenty-four hours earlier than expected.

I'd been caring for Rose's animals most of the week, but for the last two days, I had an overlap of assignments. The second client's house, at which I spent the night, was located about twenty minutes away. Vinny and I worked a schedule out where I would drive up to Rose's house for the morning ritual, and again at 5:00 to give the animals their dinner and walk the dogs. Vinny helped me by letting the dogs into the backyard for a few hours during the day, and at 10:00 for their late-night potty break. The second morning of our time-sharing responsibilities, the morning of the day Andy was to return, I'd planned to implement my end-of-assignment routine, including cleaning the rabbit's cage.

But the previous evening, Vinny telephoned me in Chester to say that he'd seen lights on in Rose's house, and had gone over to investigate. Turned out that Andy had returned home on an earlier flight! He never complained about the shape of the house, at least not to me. But I was mortified. The next morning, I went to see Andy, apologized from the bottom of my heart for the condition of the house, and returned at least twenty-five percent of what I'd been paid before they left. I also offered to help clean the house. But while Andy accepted the money, he insisted the house was no big deal.

The next time Andy and Rose hired me (and, wonder of wonders that they did!), a new latch graced the rabbit hutch making it much easier to open and close. And because I now had little fear of the bunny escaping, I had no problem cleaning it every day. In addition, after I'd earned my Veterinary Assistant certificate and learned how to handle a rabbit, bunny care became much less scary…even fun. During the warmer seasons, I carried the rabbit outside to its summer hutch where it remained until my 5:00 visit when I fed the animals their dinner and walked the dogs one more time.

Caring for Rose's animals came with a special perk: I could hand-feed the local squirrels. The unscreened porch off the kitchen sat atop a steep embankment, and squirrels would scramble up the wire mesh on the side of the house to the windowsill where they had learned that humans would offer them unshelled peanuts. Stealth was not their forte. When I heard one climbing up the mesh, I'd wait at the window with a nut held between my thumb and forefinger. The squirrel would stop, look at it, thank me, grab the goodie, and run back down the side of the house with the peanut in its mouth. Within a few minutes, the squirrel would reappear. Or maybe it was one of its kin looking to share in the bounty provided at Chez Rose. Didn't matter to me. I would dole out peanuts for half an hour at a time until the squirrel(s) had had enough or, more often, until I tore myself away to go home and get on with my real life.

I miss Rose and her family, and wish them well in New England. Wonderful people to have had as next-door neighbors, and whom several people in the immediate neighborhood knew they could count on to lend a hand if problems arose.

Seventeen

Toby, a lovable thirteen-year-old Yorkie, and Otis, a deaf, and at times wacky five-year-old Shih Tzu, together present the most challenging and gratifying of my pet-sitting assignments. These gigs allow me a glimpse into the life I once envisioned for myself had I figured out how to balance an equation, attended Michigan State University, and become a Vet Tech. Time spent with Otis and Toby is intense, but it seems to me the next best thing to working in a vet's office.

Both dogs are sweethearts and a pleasure to be with—well, after the initial minute or two of my arrival. When I first enter the house, Otis screeches from his crate in a fair imitation of how I imagine a tortured banshee might sound. Fingernails scraping across a blackboard have nothing on Otis when he's in full voice. Unconfined, he sometimes bullies little Toby, maybe because he wants a playmate and doesn't understand that Toby is too old and sick to roughhouse. Fear for Toby's safety dictates that Otis be crated in the absence of any humans to intervene on Toby's behalf.

Becky and Kevin adopted Toby through a friend of a friend who had bred their Yorkies, a one-time deal. Fourth on the waiting list, and wanting only a male, Becky and Kevin thought their chance of getting a puppy was slim at best. But some people before them on the list wanted females, so Toby found his new home in Hopatcong, New Jersey—on Christmas Eve!

Diagnosed with inoperable liver disease when two years old, Toby requires a four-times-a-day feeding schedule. Frequent small meals give his organs less to process at one time.

Toby

He can have no meat, so he eats prescription vegetarian kibble. He receives lactulose syrup orally through a syringe. The lactulose helps bind toxins and flush them from his system. In addition, Toby is syringed with Visbiome (a high-level human-grade probiotic) and Renadyl (a human-grade kidney probiotic) in an effort to keep his organs as healthy as possible.

Otis

Toby also has bladder and kidney stones for which he has undergone two bladder stone surgeries, one a medical emergency to clear a blockage, and the other a preventive measure. The stones continue to form, but his age precludes another surgery. To combat the stones and help boost his potassium citrate, he receives Ursodiol, a strong liver/kidney detoxifier.

In April 2017, Toby contracted Lyme disease and was put on a thirty-day antibiotic regimen. A second test in November provided good news: the disease was working its way out of his body, making further treatment unnecessary. Periodic testing continues to ascertain Toby's levels remain within range.

Along with his other medical issues, Toby has a partially collapsed trachea that causes him to cough frequently. Surgery, a risky option at best because of his age, again presents a poor prognosis of success.

In March 2019, Toby began sneezing several times a day violently enough that his face hit the floor, but producing no nasal discharge. Becky thought allergies caused the sneezing until it persisted for several weeks. She took him to the vet, who prescribed antibiotics. Two rounds of Clavamox—twenty days of treatment—produced no resolution to the problem. A flea/tick medication administered daily for several consecutive days to clear any possible nasal mites also failed to resolve the issue.

Concerned that Toby might have an aggressive and cancerous nasal tumor, Becky took him to a board-certified internal-medicine specialist located an hour away. A CAT scan of Toby's head to check his mouth area confirmed severe dental disease (which Becky had known about but had delayed treating because of anesthesia risks and his liver disease) and several oral nasal fistulas which were thought to cause the sneezing.

Also revealed by the CAT scan was a swollen lymph node or a tumor in his neck. A biopsy and review of results by a board-certified oncologist determined that Toby had a carotid body tumor—a rare tumor about which not a lot is known. While difficult to know for sure because of Toby's small size, the radiation oncologist thought the tumor had moved into the lymph node in Toby's neck. No doctor would attempt surgical removal of the tumor because the risk of Toby bleeding out was too high. After a full-body CAT scan to ensure that the cancer had not spread to other parts of Toby's body, the radiation oncologist suggested aggressive radiation followed by chemotherapy treatments. Three radiation treatments on three consecutive days. Becky chose not to put Toby through chemotherapy because she thought chemo and liver disease were a dangerous combination. Three months after the radiation treatments, a chest X-ray revealed that the cancer had not spread. Toby will undergo another full-body CAT scan in November 2019 to determine how much the radiation shrunk the tumor, and to see if there is any evidence that the cancer has spread to other parts of his body.

After his radiation treatments, Becky took Toby to an oncologist who specializes in holistic medicine and treatments, and who put him on several supplements for his cancer, liver disease, bladder/kidney stones, and collapsing trachea.

In July 2019, Toby was stable enough with normal bloodwork results to undergo the required dental work. He had nine teeth extracted, and several oral nasal fistulas repaired at Blue Pearl Pet Hospital in Paramus, New Jersey. One tooth could not be extracted because the risk of fracturing his jaw was too great. Instead, the tooth was packed in an attempt to stimulate its reattachment to the jaw. Toby came through the procedure with flying colors, and wanted to eat dry food as soon as soon as he returned home from Blue Pearl! He will be rechecked in January to determine whether or not the tooth in question is responding to treatment. If not, it will be extracted at that time.

Toby continues to have bloodwork and chest X-rays done every three months and continues to visit the holistic veterinarian.

Kevin and Becky adopted Otis as a puppy from a rescue group in April 2014 after losing Duke, a mixed-breed rescue, to kidney disease earlier that year. A few weeks after bringing Otis home, Kevin and Becky brought the dogs with them to spend Easter with family.

Her dad noticed that Otis didn't respond to loud noises. Neither banging a pot near his ear nor chirping the fire alarm, both sounds which caused Toby to flee, had any effect upon Otis other than to cause him to look around in bewilderment at the ruckus happening around him. If his deafness detracts from Otis's personality and bouts of craziness, I don't notice it.

Otis has been diagnosed with irritable bowel syndrome. Pediasure, along with Pepcid and Prednisone, help manage acid build-up in his stomach. But Becky has strong reservations about giving Otis steroids for extended periods of time without noticeable improvement to his condition, and has devoted hours to extensive research on natural alternatives. As a result, Otis is being weaned off the Prednisone, and now receives the same vegetarian kibble as Toby, along with hemp oil, slippery elm, and Visbiome.

The regimen for the dogs' care continues while Becky and Kevin are away, and, I spend lots of time on the floor with one pup or the other syringing different potions and charms into their mouths. (I invoke Harry Potter speak because making up Toby's and Otis's meals—and encouraging them to eat—equates to magic for me.) I get to engage in all the trench warfare against doggie illness that a would-be animal technician could desire or handle. Each meal takes at least forty-five minutes from start to finish, including down time while fourteen and thirty pieces of kibble, respectively, soak in two cups of microwaved-for-thirty-seconds water. These details may sound obsessive, but they are derived from math teacher Becky's careful calculation of protein grams. For instance, it is believed that when Toby receives too much protein, ammonia builds up in his brain and causes odd behavior like rubbing his face on the carpet and/or nausea. The mealtime process continues after I "serve" the meals and wait for Otis and Toby to decide if they want to eat, or if they want me to coax them with hand-feeding. And then there are the supplements that vary in content and amount with each meal. A ml of this, two drops of that, half a capsule of something else, a syringe for this, a syringe for that, mix it all up, draw into syringe, sit on floor next to dog, cradle and lift his head, insert syringe into corner of dog's mouth, slowly depress plunger. Sometimes one of the dogs (never both during the same meal) like the concoction I serve up, and accept it without hesitation. Other times, coercion to accept the syringe becomes a time-consuming messy struggle.

I so applaud Becky and Kevin who commit to this painstaking routine day in and day out. It's clear they spare no effort or expense in keeping Toby and Otis as healthy and comfortable as possible, and it is my privilege and pleasure to take over the critical care of these wonderful little dogs.

Eighteen

Toby and Otis share their sleeping space with me when I care for them, and allow me to snuggle under the blankets, and maybe dream good dreams. Who remembers dreams?

One time, a gentle but persistent pawing on my arm from Toby, who always claims a spot up near my head, awakened me. I opened my eyes enough to see that the clock read 4:30. Sorry, Toby, too early for breakfast. And I rolled over. A trembling bundle beside me kept me awake long enough to see a flash through my closed eyes. Followed by thunder! My all-important ear plugs, inserted before I'd gone to sleep, had done their job and prevented me from hearing the boomers while I slept. I turned back to the quaking Yorkie who doesn't like thunder, but I assumed liked the idea of wearing earplugs less, and ensconced him in the crook of my arm. Once tucked under the comforter away from his monsters in the night, all was good.

The following morning began with unusual behavior for the dogs, and developed into a ghost story of sorts kind of day.

The first bit of strangeness occurred when Otis and Toby both ate their breakfast without requiring coercion from me. Oh, happy day! But I kept an eye on their eating from my vantage spot on the living room ottoman to make certain that they finished, or almost finished, their meal. Then without warning or fanfare of any kind, Otis slowly and simultaneously raised both his hind legs and posed in a kind of handstand for a split second, after which he lowered his legs and continued eating. I returned my eyeballs to their sockets, blinked several times, and wondered if I'd just seen what I thought I'd seen. A screwy performance even for Otis.

Breakfast finished, and while I washed the dishes and various syringes, measuring cups, and other assorted paraphernalia called into service for preparing the dogs' battery of supplements, the boys exited through the doggie door to check out the warmth of the sun on the deck, and sniff the early morning air.

Within a couple of minutes, Otis rocketed back into the kitchen, raced into the living room, jumped onto and off of both sofas and the one armchair, careened back through the kitchen, and onto the deck—only to re-emerge seconds later at the same breakneck speed with an occasional happy yip, and repeat his previous lap, taking one small detour to jump playfully at my legs. He repeated the equivalent of a NASCAR road course three or four times before bounding one final time onto the back of the living room easy chair from where he could observe the goings on in his immediate neighborhood. I'd never seen the five-year-old Otis so joyful. Chalked his high spirits up to the gorgeous morning and the promise of a fabulous day ahead. Animals can sense excellent weather, as well as bad. Maybe something to do with the rise and fall of barometric pressure. Whatever. Otis's jubilance made my heart happy.

Six or seven hours later, after the dogs' second meal, Otis returned to his favorite perch on the back of the living room easy chair, and fell asleep. I acknowledged Toby's request to be picked up and placed on the seat cushions of the same chair where he, too, fell asleep. The two of them looked so beyond sweet that I took a picture of them and texted it to Mommy Becky.

~ Stormie's Heart ~

Becky's return text surprised me. She wanted to know if there was a third dog in the picture laying on the steps. I looked at the photo and laughed. The chair was covered with a throw that had a large picture of a Yorkie printed on it, and had slid out of position in such a way that it may have looked like Otis and Toby were asleep on the stairs. When I responded that the "third dog" was the blanket, Becky texted back that in the photo, the dog looked just like their deceased dog, Duke. I looked again at the picture and was startled to see that the blanket no longer looked like a blanket. Indeed, it appeared to have changed to reveal a living three-dimensional dog lying beneath and to the left of Toby. So much so, that one of its ears cut a triangular wedge into the chair's cushion above it. The "third dog" even cast a shadow where a shadow would have been cast, given those of Toby and Otis. And the cushions upon which Toby slept appeared to have levitated to accommodate the "third dog" underneath them.

Becky then texted that she would "love to have one more day with Duke, and see all three boys (even though Otis and Duke had never met) play together while young and healthy."

I replayed in my mind the events of earlier that morning, and found it easy to believe that maybe it wasn't the weather after all that had Otis so excited. In an attempt to establish a possible rational explanation for the metamorphosis of the photo (even though I know for certain that rational explanations don't exist for some events), I went over to the easy chair and attempted to "rebuild" the photo that had revealed a "third dog." I moved the blanket and cushions every which way. I held the camera at different angles. Not even close to the image I'd forwarded to Becky.

So maybe Duke had been there after all, and only the camera lens caught it. I've had too many encounters with the paranormal to discount the possibility of spirit visitation, even from that of a dog. There's stuff out there that we don't understand, can't explain, and can't prove or disprove—a kind of twilight zone—a mystic dimension in which ESP, ghosts, and other unexplainable phenomena occur. I consider myself fortunate to be among the relative few from our three-dimensional plane of existence who sometimes catch a glimpse of the alternative universe, that magical realm in which science gains no foothold.

Nineteen

March 2018 produced a blue moon and came in like a lion following a Nor'easter on February 27. Within ten days of the February storm, March birthed two additional Nor'easters transforming what had been a mild winter into one for the books.

FIRST STORM

The February 27th storm dumped seven to eight inches of wind-driven snow across the northeast and caused us to lose power for three full days. An invitation early on during the second day from friends who hadn't lost power, and Vinny sent me packing while he remained at home with only our portable generator to provide electricity. Road crews worked round the clock in frigid temperatures to restore power as soon as possible, but the ambient hums and clicks of electrical gadgets remained silent while the temperature in the house plummeted to forty-seven degrees.

And Mother Nature's second punch loomed imminent and large when I was slated to be with Duncan the Corgi.

SECOND STORM

I'd planned to get to Nancie's house by 7:00 in the evening so I would be with Duncan in the downstairs apartment when she left the house for an early flight next morning. But it had snowed all day with no end in sight. I texted Nancie. Did she still want me to come over that night? Yes. Her driveway had been plowed. Okay, but I'd rather get there during early afternoon after the plows had made another pass down our street, and before it got dark. No problem. So next time the plow pushed its way up our street, Vinny put the snow blower to work clearing our driveway. And the snow continued to fall.

In the past, Vinny had always followed me in his van for the ten-minute drive to Nancie's house so he could help carry my luggage down the steps to the apartment. That night, we agreed that he would ride with me in my four-wheel-drive Xterra because that vehicle was better in snow than his large utility van. But I insisted on driving, and against his better judgment, Vinny agreed. After taking longer than five minutes to crawl almost one block to the bottom of our street, I told Vinny, "You drive." We arrived at Nancie's house without incident, and Vinny drove my SUV home with plans to return it to me the next day.

I spent a couple of hours with Nancie in her living room while she manned her telephone talking to concerned friends, checking on flights, and cajoling her driver into a commitment to drive her to the airport the next morning. The last thing she said to me before I went downstairs to the apartment with Duncan was, "Things have a way of working out." Her conviction, though strong, seemed misplaced to me. I went to sleep doubting that Nancie would make it out of the driveway the following day, much less to the airport. And should Fate smile a bright enough smile upon her long enough for her to arrive at Newark Airport, well, I hoped she'd thought to pack a good book to read while all the delayed and canceled flights waited for runways to be cleared of snow.

When I awoke next morning at 6:00, all was still. I took Duncan out for his early morning pee and romp in the snow, and noticed half-covered tire tracks in the driveway. Were they there last night when Vinny and I arrived? Were they made by my truck? I didn't think so, but… Continued absolute silence from the house above the apartment when Duncan and I returned.

I have no qualms about being alone in someone else's house while pet sitting, but not knowing for sure if I was the only one in the house set my nerves on edge. I toyed with the idea of calling Nancie on her cell to find out where she was, but hesitated. Didn't want to chance waking her if she were still home. Instead, I listened hard for any hint of her presence—footsteps, running water—and kept a close eye on Duncan whose hearing was better than mine, and who would react to any sound issuing from somewhere other than the apartment. But I heard and saw nothing to belie my sole presence in the house.

Nancie called me later that morning; she had arrived in South Carolina…and on time! Hers had been the first flight out of Newark Airport. I recalled what she'd said about things working out, and I couldn't help smiling to myself. Would the universe have dared cross Nancie?

Upon concluding my assignment with Duncan, I returned home where the caprice of March enjoyed a *hurrah!* at our expense when Vinny turned on the outside water from the basement so I could hose all the salt, dirt and general gunkiness off my car. I went downstairs to grab my keys and move the truck from under its protective tarp. Heard what sounded like torrential rain. Opened the connecting door between the laundry room and garage, and looked outside. Cloudy, gray, cold…but no rain. I figured the "rain" I'd heard was Vinny taking it upon himself to help me by hosing down the back of the truck before I backed it out onto the driveway.

But when he stalked into the garage, grumpy faced and growling, something told me that this was one time he wasn't looking for a Wookiee treat in exchange for going above and beyond in his desire to please me. He was loaded for bear, the bear in this case being a blown elbow joint in the pipe that fed the hose. I couldn't see the broken pipe because it was on the far side of the Trans Am, but we (well, Vinny) moved the car, the snow blower, the lawn mower, and miscellaneous garage stuff outside, and revealed a soaked floor. A trip to Home Depot later, some smashed knuckles later, some sailor's parrot vocabulary later, and the wee elbow joint tucked deep in a corner of the garage was repaired.

But my truck, my poor truck, remained encrusted in winter's dirty leftovers until the next morning when I, looking and feeling like I'd lost my marbles in Neverland, moved the Xterra from under the tarp into the mist and cold and spitting rain for a much-needed bath.

THIRD STORM

Then began an assignment in Dover on Easter Saturday during which yet another Nor'easter had been predicted. I'd already assured Mary that should she become snowbound in North Carolina, I'd be willing and able to extend my time with her Warren.

The snow arrived Sunday night and continued into the following day. And the little Bichon raced down the two flights of stairs first thing Monday morning when he saw me reach for his harness, and waited for me inside the door to the street. I leashed Warren, opened the door, and ventured out into a snow-filled setting that fell universes short of the lyrical lines in "Winter Wonderland." Several parked salt trucks lined the street—engines running at a volume that drowned out the whistles of incoming and outgoing trains at the station across the street, and stinking up the air with their diesel-infused exhausts. At least three inches of blackened snow had collected behind each truck. I took a deep breath, gagged on the truck fumes, and resolved to hold my breath from then on as long as possible.

But Warren, never having been privy to the pastoral winter tableaux of Currier & Ives, enjoyed the city snow and gamboled on the as-yet-unplowed sidewalk from pole to pole, marking each one according to his doggy instinct. When we rounded the corner into the center of town, the scene shifted to one of early-morning controlled chaos. A moderate flow of vehicles stopped and started between the traffic lights at every intersection. Pedestrians, most clutching their coffee cups in both hands, chatted to one another, greeted me (*"Hola!"*), and hurried along plowed sidewalks to their Monday destinations. Snow continued to fall. But this snow, as compared to that outside Mary's apartment door, was "quiet" and white except for what little lay in the street.

Warren and I observed this dual-sided early-spring spectacle, he in his warm lamb-like coat, and I in my cold wet sneakers for having forgotten to pack my boots two days ago, and having also forgotten to ask Vinny to bring them with him the day before when on his Godiva-chocolate-bunny run. I scare myself sometimes!

Warren

Winter-like spring continued outside with a cloud-obscured sun and blustery winds that made the cold temperatures feel even colder. But indoors, the day passed in cozy comfort. Warren investigated the Easter basket left for him by Mary, and I gnawed the ears off my own chocolate treat while I worked at my laptop.

At dinnertime, Warren moved to his kitchen bed (as opposed to his bed in the living room, the bathroom, and every other room in the apartment) so he could be near the action wherever it happened. I preheated the oven to four hundred degrees and set about preparing some asparagus for roasting. But I could find nothing flat on which to spread them. Ah, the broiling pans in the compartment under the oven. *Yes!* It didn't register until a picosecond too late that Mary has a gas oven unlike ours, which is electric. The "drawer" below our oven stays cool when the oven is hot. Not so with a gas oven. Opened the drawer, reached in, and grabbed a fast hold of a four-hundred-degree hot metal sheet pan with both hands. *Yeowww!*

Pain exploded through my reddened fingertips, but I had the presence of mind to run them under cold water after releasing the hot pan. Somewhere, maybe during my EMT training, I'd heard that cold water provides the quickest and best means of retarding a burn injury. Keep the injured body part submerged in cold water until the pain stops. So long as pain continues, damage continues. After several minutes of following this "treatment," including putting my hands into the freezer and on top of frozen packages of meat and vegetables, the pain did not abate. I saw no blistering, but something told me I'd suffered at least second-degree burns, and that blistering would appear before long.

While searching Mary's closets for cortisone cream, I found a bottle of Banana Boat "Aloe After Sun." Looked at it with some skepticism, but thought, 'what can it hurt?' Aloe is lauded everywhere as possessing near-magical healing properties. Massaged some of the lotion into my hands, and I mean to tell you that potion stopped the searing pain in my fingers on contact! No lie. Another application before falling asleep. I awoke the following morning to unblistered fingers that no longer screamed in agony, even when exposed to hot shower water. Move over, cortisone, and make room for Banana Boat!

Twenty

When not pet sitting, I toss an assortment of nuts and seeds to the local squirrels, chipmunks, groundhogs, and birds every morning or afternoon from our dining room window onto the patio. It gives me a sense of connection to nature when I click my tongue against the roof of my mouth, and several squirrels respond within minutes, sometimes seconds, and cascade down the trees to await food. A few squirrels have learned that if they hang out on or near the front stoop, or under the dining room window, there's a good chance peanuts and sunflower seeds will materialize. In the evening after dark, I offer bread and leftover dinner vegetables to raccoons, possums, and other night critters. And when the ground is covered with deep snow, Vinny clears our patio and plows a path to it for hungry creatures.

One morning, I glanced outside and saw a healthy-looking fox chowing down on the peanuts just outside the glass doors opening onto the patio. Who knew foxes ate peanuts? Thrilled to see a fox for the first time, I began to look for her every day. My diligence was rewarded, and I saw her several times after the initial sighting. And the joy of seeing her never diminished, no matter how often she visited.

Fox

I threw some saltines to her to which she turned up her nose. Picky, picky, picky. Then, after determining that foxes were canine (as opposed to feline), I bought a bag of Beneful dry food for her in hopes that she would like it so much that she'd return to our house more often. While I never saw her eat the kibble, the dish I put out in the evening was always empty by morning.

Then, the morning after the first of the three March Nor'easters, I checked the fox's food dish, saw it was empty, but didn't see any fox pawprints in the snow around it. Figured she stopped by for an early dinner before the snow ended overnight.

That evening, I again filled the bowl and left it for the fox. And, again, by the next morning, the food had all been eaten. Lots of pawprints around the bowl this time, but not those of a fox.

A review of our motion-sensitive camera revealed a hungry raccoon raiding the Beneful bowl. Because I wanted to save the Beneful for the fox next time she came around, I stopped putting the food out at night. But we never saw the fox again, and I hoped she made it through that wicked March—maybe moved on to a more sheltered den.

Twenty-one

The March 2018 barrage of Nor'easters ran their course just in time to usher in the second full moon (Worm Moon) of the month. And by the fourth week of March, warmer temperatures and sunshine had converted snow-covered grassy areas to sloppy bogs in which I could schlepp during my upcoming assignment with Buddy, Keno, Fred, and Gene.

Anticipation of time in Montville always calmed me. But I awoke the day I was to begin the current gig with a borderline panic attack after having fallen asleep the night before disturbed by the occurrence of "one of those feelings." As it turned out, that wee voice, that Delphian voice, which almost always knows what it's talking about was right on. The oodles of little things gone wrong that ensued up to and during my assignment brought me to the brink of consulting an astrology book for a crash course in "How to Do Life during a Blue Moon."

The panic attack wannabe gnawed at my gut, and I responded by dithering around the house and getting next to nothing accomplished, which resulted in my running behind schedule for my departure to Montville. Further complicating matters, traffic congested in tangled knots as I attempted to balance making up time on the road with avoiding any random but vigilant radar detector in some police cruiser. I arrived at the house not late enough to be an issue, and Debbie told me Keno had been sick. A grim start for any assignment.

Debbie and Phil left for their getaway and returned less than ten minutes later because Debbie had forgotten her water. No big deal. Just one more little tick out of the ordinary as the universe continued to set my world in "tilt" mode.

After taking the dogs outside for a quick potty break, I remembered I needed to call Vinny to let him know that I'd arrived safely at my destination. But a couple of skin tags on my back were screaming to be scratched with my handy-dandy little metal rake. Nagging disease ratcheted up to a nail-biting cold sweat when, after searching in vain for the scratcher, I came to the incontrovertible realization that I'd left it at home. Legions of imaginary ants mobilized on my back within seconds.

Frantic, I went to grab my cell phone to call Vinny and beg him to drive over with the back scratcher. But I couldn't find the phone either. Could I possibly have left home without my phone AND my rake? I called Vinny from the house phone and learned that things had gone haywire in his buddy's world, as well as mine.

Danny had rented a car to drive to Illinois from New York to pick up another car on which he'd bid in an online auction. He had been told he could show up anytime to take possession of the vehicle; no phone call necessary. After Danny had driven almost two hundred miles into the trip, he thought it wise to call just to tell them he was on his way…as a courtesy. In response to his call, "Any week but this one. The girl who does the paperwork is out this week." *Grrr!*

I hung up with Vinny after leaving him with non-negotiable instructions to search the house for my phone and rake…*stat!* And then I backed up against the nearest wall and sought to neutralize the juiced-up nerve cells on my back. A modicum of relief, and I thought I might distract myself from my agony with a stint on the computer.

Padded into a guest room where the laptops lived (hadn't bought my own yet), sat down at the desk, and prepared for what I hoped would be an engrossing-to-the-exclusion-of-all-physical-torments time of productivity until Vinny arrived with my "preferred weapon" against my itchy back. But because I didn't see Debbie's ThinkPad (my laptop of choice), I logged onto Phil's laptop, and…*Damn!* The computer wouldn't accept the password that I'd listed in my Montville file. I noticed a thin flat gizmo sticking out about a quarter of an inch from the right side of the laptop, and thinking it was the computer equivalent of a SIM card, pushed it in all the way. The click I heard when it slid into place sounded too final, too loud…almost ominous. Dismay washed over me as I attempted to remove whatever instrument of corruption—perhaps some rogue circuit board programmed to erase all memory—that I'd inflicted upon the laptop. But try as I might, I could not dislodge the accursed device.

And then I saw my go-to laptop, the faithful ThinkPad that had been buried beneath some papers. Too late. My creative jets had cooled, and I was left with Column B for further distraction: television.

Vinny called the house phone later in the evening, but no joy. Neither my cell nor my rake was anywhere to be found.

Exhaustion by day's end from anxiety, from boredom, and from searching again and again through my luggage for the missing phone and back scratcher prevented me from my usual therapeutic reading in bed. My brain seized up and refused to focus. Lulled myself to sleep instead with what I could remember of the Twenty-Third Psalm, along with Scarlett O'Hara's immortal words, "Tomorrow is another day."

And "tomorrow" did indeed prove itself to be another day as I noticed that Keno, without question, felt better. His eyes had lost their lackluster appearance, and his energy level had returned to normal. I later discovered my cell phone tucked away within a deep fold of my handbag, and the back scratcher lurked in a never-used compartment of luggage. Feeling too relieved to question how I'd missed finding either implement the day before despite checking and rechecking the same places, I chalked the whole thing up to the universe playing games with me…again.

And Vinny, after hearing from me how life had returned to a more even keel, felt safe coming to visit me empty-handed to look at the "thing" I'd wedged into Phil's laptop. Turned out to be the CD drive. *Duh!* So no emergency there, which further freed up my mind and granted me some productive time at the ThinkPad's keyboard.

And Debbie texted me that, after the initial hiccup of forgetting her water, she and Phil had arrived in Philadelphia for her son's wedding without mishap.

Only Danny's circumstances remained beyond repair. He had no choice but to return home to New York in his rental car and look forward to the prospect of driving to Illinois the following week—when the waning blue moon of March would hold less sway over life's craps table.

Twenty-two

I can get along with almost any animal. But there are those poor damaged creatures whose chemical makeup or psychological scars render them forever at odds with humans, even those potentially loving caregivers. Muffin was such an animal: an orange and gray calico cat, born into the horrific conditions of a kitty mill, and sold to a mall pet store from where she was purchased by Adrienne and Pete, and brought to her forever home.

Despite evidencing typical kitten behavior early on in her new home, Muffin's confidence and playfulness deteriorated into fear and increased periods of isolation. What triggered the demise of the young cat's personality? Her humans don't know, but admit to having had her declawed when she was a kitten, a decision they regret and vow never to inflict upon another cat.

Adrienne and Pete later bought an Australian Shepherd (Tara) and another kitten (Kevin), both from the pet store where they'd gotten Muffin. Muffin hated the newcomers. Tara and Kevin reciprocated by chasing and otherwise tormenting Muffin, who sometimes sought solace in the arms of Adrienne, the only living being of any species she would tolerate.

Adrienne and I met at a Ladies Bible Study and developed a casual friendship. One day, having learned that I was a pet sitter, she asked if I'd consider caring for her three animals. Sure! Let's schedule a meet-and-greet.

The now eleven-year-old Muffin lay curled up on a bed the first time I saw her, and she watched me with wary eyes as I approached her with Adrienne. "She's going to hiss," Adrienne warned. But to my surprise and Adrienne's amazement, she let me pet her and scritch her under the chin. "Pete! Stormie is petting Muffin!" Feeling more than a little smug, I left the house confident and thinking to myself: I got this!

The day arrived when my assignment with Muffin and her housemates was to begin, and as prearranged, Adrienne and Pete had already left. I entered the house to Tara's incessant barking, Kevin's supervision of the scene from the dining room table, and Muffin's anticipated absence. After unpacking my things and calming Tara with a walk around the block, I wandered around the house in search of Muffin and found her under a bed. Attempts to coax her out to me were met with a low, deep-throated growl. Okay. So much for making instant nice with Muffin.

When the time came for me to descend into the basement to feed the cats, I hoped Muffin would shelve her hostility long enough to venture out from under the bed and join Kevin downstairs for dinner. Kevin beat me down the stairs, and jumped up on the washing machine waiting for me to fill his dish. No sign of Muffin.

But as I bent to retrieve her dish from the floor after having fed Kevin, I heard a hiss. I turned in the direction of the sound and saw Muffin crouching behind some boxes a couple of feet from where I stooped, glaring at me with all the hatred of a demon from hell. I reached for the dish, and the hiss became a growl as she swiped at me with a paw. *Hmm.* How to feed the little beastie. I located a broom in the corner and attempted to maneuver the bowl closer to me and away from Muffin. More snarls and paw action, this time accompanied by spitting. I experimented with using the broom to nudge Muffin away from me and my hand. Bad move. Muffin's fury reached a fever pitch. She leapt onto a pile of boxes about five feet high and screamed at me, sounding every bit a mountain lion. Kevin turned tail and fled. Tara raced back and forth overhead in agitation during the fracas. I tried to shut out the sounds of what sounded like a *Wild Kingdom* soundtrack echoing through the confines of the small basement while I concentrated on feeding a house cat morphed into a would-be killer cougar. How could such a small animal produce such prolonged ear-piercing volume? While Muffin screamed at me from on high, I grabbed the opportunity to fill her bowl, half expecting her to spring from the boxes onto my back as she tapped into the killer instinct of her undomesticated and much larger kin.

    I've cared for Muffin and her housemates several times since that inaugural visit. She maintains a steadfast, self-imposed, sad, and solitary existence, but she and I have reached a fragile compromise: I ascertain that she is nowhere nearby when filling her food and water bowls; she allows me to persevere in my initial delusion. Yeah, I got this!

Twenty-three

I came to know Rockey through the recommendation of Nancie, Duncan's owner, who was referred to me by our mutual dental hygienist. Rockey, a fourteen-year-old Corgi mix in whom I could see the "mix" but had difficulty picking out the Corgi, was a sweet animal who had lost most of his hearing and was developing cataracts when I met him. He had two Hindu humans, Prema and Sam. Prema always greeted me with a hug and engaged me in conversation as soon as I arrived at the house while Sam tended to hang back.

Rockey's house was an interesting one in which to stay. Hindu artifacts everywhere. And a bunch of kitchen utensils that I didn't use—didn't even know what some of them were. The cupboards contained food that I'd never bought.

I learned bits of Indian culture from Prema, the first being at the conclusion of my initial assignment with Rockey. When she paid me, I reached for the money with my left hand (I do everything with my left hand except shift the manual transmission in my truck), but Prema insisted that I accept it from my right. Tradition in the Hindu religion dictates that one always gives with, and receives from, the right hand as a reciprocal blessing, and as an indication of mutual respect.

Rockey ate four small meals a day of blended apples, carrots, pears, potatoes, broccoli, bananas, and other goodies. Prema, smart lady, prepared several portions at once in her food processor and froze them until needed. My job consisted of thawing four of the prepared packets ahead of time, warming one

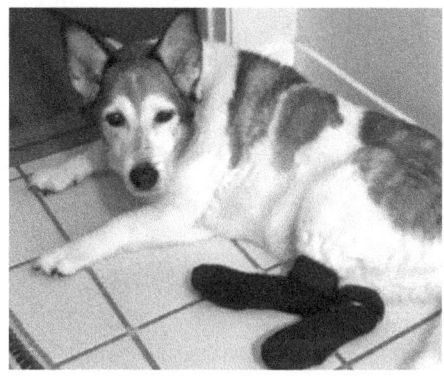

Rockey with socks

in the microwave for a few seconds before feeding time, emptying it into a food bowl, and putting it on the floor. When he was awake, Rockey came right for it. But like most older dogs, he slept a lot, so I sometimes brought his food to him and waved it in front of his nose for him to smell. Within minutes of opening his eyes, he ambled into the kitchen for his meal. I try to eat a diet as healthy as Rockey's, but foods like dark chocolate, Cherry Garcia ice cream, and rare steak stonewall my good intentions at every turn.

Despite Rockey's cataracts and increasing deafness, he recognized a T-Rex when he saw one on television. A commercial for the latest and greatest *Jurassic Park* movie aired one evening, and Rockey jumped from the easy chair in which he'd been ensconced, ran to the tv, and barked until the scary dinosaurs went away. *Oh, there's the Corgi!*

Rockey had also developed some sort of itchy infection in his ears that was treated with drops, which Rockey hated. He ran away when he saw me approaching with the dreaded little white bottle, so I took to moistening a paper towel with a few drops, hiding the bottle in my pocket, and massaging the medicine into his ears before sneaking in a couple of drops. It made me sad to see his eyes fill with reproach at the way I'd tricked him, but I couldn't figure an easier way to administer the medication. And to add insult to injury, I had to put a cone on him for at least an hour afterward so he couldn't scratch and prevent the drops from doing their job. He submitted to the collar with a resignation that tore at my heartstrings, and I wished there was a way to assure him that I didn't mean to torture him. I hated seeing him in such misery, and looked forward to removing the collar almost as much as he anticipated being released from it.

One month after my initial assignment with Rockey, I readied for a second gig with him. Ominous signals from the get-go, beginning as I drove down Route 10 at sixty miles per hour to avoid being run over by traffic on the posted fifty-mile-per-hour highway. The first time I hit the brakes, they chattered to such an extent that the truck vibrated and scared me half to death. A visit to the service station a few days later revealed that I needed to replace my brake rotors. This procedure, coupled with the fact that my trusty fourteen-year-old Xterra had begun spending way too much time in the repair shop, brought me face to face with the daunting dilemma of either continuing to replace parts of the undercarriage one by one, or steeling myself for a venture into the sordid world of auto sales in search of another Xterra (or any decent SUV) with a standard transmission. Much wringing of hands as I wrestled with my choices.

When I arrived at the house with jangled nerves, Prema met me at the door with her usual welcoming smile and hug. She called to the nearly deaf Rockey who was lying on the sofa with Sam and couldn't see me, "Look who's here! It's Stormie!" Rockey jumped up and trotted over to me with a big smile on his face. Prema's and Sam's faces registered amazement. Rockey almost never acknowledged a visitor with such demonstrative behavior unless it was someone he knew. With most newcomers, he kept his distance and barked until he felt comfortable enough to let a visitor pet him. Maybe he remembered me from six weeks before, even though I had been with him only ten days. Whatever. His response made me feel good and mitigated the dread I'd harbored since having my teeth rattled while driving on Route 10.

~ Stormie's Heart ~

Because I get anal about kitchen cleanliness, the first thing I did after Prema and Sam left, and after tending to Rockey, was put dirty coffee cups and a couple of soiled dishes into the dishwasher and wipe down the counter. I then rinsed all the leftover food in the sink down the drain, flipped the garbage disposal switch on, and flipped it off at once when I heard a protesting racket. Peered down the drain to see what I could see, and saw the handle of some piece of flatware poking out. I hadn't seen any forks or spoons in the sink when I cleaned it. But as luck would have it, the teaspoon I extricated from the drain suffered little harm from its encounter with the whirring disposal blades.

Rockey, like almost every other dog I know, loved to go for walks. Whenever he saw me pick up his leash (always first thing in the morning before the summer heat and humidity grew oppressive), he kind of pranced around and lifted both front feet off the floor in an attempt to jump. Vestiges of his younger days. I allowed him to pick his own pace when we walked, which was spry enough at the beginning of our outings. And he always gave me the impression that he'd like to walk further than the usual block and a half, but by the time we returned home, he appeared to have nothing left and collapsed in his bed after I'd given him his treat.

Most evenings, we enjoyed a short time of R & R together, during which he celebrated his inner puppy. We'd engage in a good tug o' war, or he'd chase and retrieve his plush bone at a lope after I'd wrested it from him and tossed it down the hall.

OUTSIDE AFTER DARK

Rockey took his late-night potty break on the deck around 10:00 before I went to bed. One night, instead of jumping up as he always did when he saw me walk to the sliding glass doors, he remained where he was on the floor and just looked at me. I had to "persuade" him to go out. And it was only with clear misgiving that he submitted to my will. I could almost hear him mumbling about how mad he was about the whole ordeal.

Once outside, I slid the door shut to prevent armies of moths, beetles, and unidentified nighttime bugs from invading my stronghold, and waited for Rockey to do his thing. Mission accomplished. I turned to reenter the house, but the sliding door wouldn't budge because the latch on the inside had slid down from the "open" position to the "locked" position. And all the windows that I could reach were locked. *Aaaargh!*

So it was about 10:15 on a warm but pitch-black night, the stars obscured by clouds. And I'm hanging outside barefoot on the deck with no cell phone, no keys, and no garage door combination because Prema had told me before she left that she didn't remember it. To further complicate things, Vinny, my go-to solver of all glitches, was in Upstate New York on a well-deserved fishing weekend with his buddies.

My one option: Knock on a neighbor's door and ask them to call the police for me. As I picked my way around the house in the darkness, mindful that any one of the leaves brushing against my ankles could be poison ivy, I giggled with relief that I at least was wearing a pair of shorts. Most days, I'd have traded my daytime clothes for nothing but a long T-shirt as soon as it got dark. I rang the doorbell of a nearby house in which lights were still on, and saw a man peer out a window that flanked the door. I backed away to show him I meant no harm at 5' tall and 103 pounds. The Good Samaritan then opened his door, listened to my story, and called the police for me. I returned to the deck to retrieve Rockey, whose anxious barking had increased in volume and frequency. Together, we walked to the front of the house to await rescue.

Within minutes, a patrol car drove up the cul-de-sac with a spotlight shining brightly enough to illuminate everything within a three-block radius. I was surprised to see only one officer in the car given recent occurrences of cop ambushes. He got out of the cruiser, asked me a battery of routine questions, and then followed Rockey and me through those mysterious leafy things back to the deck.

Unable to budge the glass door that had no handle on the outside, he asked me about the owners of the house. I gave him their names and told him they were in Texas until the end of the week. Okay, he would return to the patrol car to see if he could contact them. I sat down on the deck with a concerned and confused Rockey, and tried to figure out how we were going to get out of this one. I had just taken a deep cleansing breath after committing the whole situation to God for Him to work out when the cop appeared at the glass slider from inside the kitchen and opened the door for me. He'd reached the owners and obtained the garage door combination from Sam.

So forty minutes from the time I'd convinced Rockey that, against his better judgment, it was a good idea to venture outside onto the deck, we were back inside where I was left to consider the real possibility that I was not the only one in the house who possessed a strong working sixth sense.

It wasn't until I'd completed the assignment, returned home, and was leafing through Rockey's file searching for any additions and corrections that I saw I'd had the combination all along, having been given it by Sam during our meet-and-greet several months earlier. Because I'd never used it, I'd forgotten I had it. Called upon an irrefutable rationalization to console myself over my stupidity: I hadn't committed the code to memory, so the information in the file would have done me no good anyway once I'd locked myself out of the house.

COMMUNICATION BREAKDOWN

Sometimes, it's the client rather than the animal that gives a pet sitter fits. The following recounts a text dialog over the period of a month between Prema and myself. Miscommunication constitutes an understatement.

Prema's initial text in early June: Are you available July 8-12?

Response: Yes

A few days later:

Her text: Are you available July 4-12?

Response: Yes. What time would you like me to arrive on the fourth?

Her text: Any time before noon.

Response: I'll be there at 11:00.

Later in June:

Her text: We'll see you between 10:00-11:00.

Response: Would you prefer I arrive at 10:00? (Trying to be an intuitive pet sitter)

Her text: Whatever is easiest. Don't rush.

July 2:

Her text: Could you arrive between 7:00-7:30 a.m.? We want to leave by 8:00.

Response: That might be a problem because you live thirty to forty minutes from me in the direction of New York, and I don't like driving in rush hour traffic. Would you be okay with me arriving after you've gone?"

Her text: No problem. We'll feed Rockey his breakfast. If you could arrive in time to give him his noon meal."

July 3:

Her text: We will be in NYC July 4-6, but will be coming home at night and returning to the City the following day, sometimes as late as 3:00 in the afternoon. Will be home very early in the morning on July 7, and will depart for Canada July 8 early in the morning.

What? I admit to feeling like I'd been played. This was the first I'd heard about Prema and Sam coming home while I was in their house, and I was left with a difficult choice: Either I would have to drive home every night and return the next morning (something I would never have consented to do had I known about my clients' plans ahead of time), remain home all day on July 7, and cut my fee accordingly. OR I would have to subject myself to living in someone else's house while the owners were home, and suffering the awkward situation of being neither a real friend nor an invited guest…and avoiding going bonkers from self-imposed solitary confinement to my room for twenty-four hours without television or computer. Couldn't even begin to wrap my mind around the logistics involving meals. A verbal discussion between us ensued in which Prema said they'd be home after midnight those nights, and she would be working on July 7. I could carry on as if they weren't home because they would be sleeping most of the time.

HOME, BUT NOT ALONE

So an interesting and uneasy scenario loomed—and a first for me: pet sitting while the owners leave the house sometime during the day and return home late at night. I sweat bullets in anticipation of trying to maintain a balance between respecting Sam and Prema's privacy and living my own life. And as with most things, the reality of the situation spun out nowhere near as terribly as I'd anticipated. Our brains excel at blowing events yet to happen out of proportion, and most things unfold far less scary than we imagine.

Sam and Prema did all they could to accommodate me. Sam went so far as to give up his office so I could work on my laptop, which I'd set up in his study. And he forfeited some television time while I watched *Beauty and the Beast* DVDs. Ah, the combination of fantasy and romance in that television series…

During those times when the three of us were awake and in the kitchen or living room together, we got to know each other better. I welcomed the opportunity to bridge the gap between Sam and me by helping him send a video from Facebook to another person.

The adventure did have its moments—like the day Rockey and I returned from our early morning walk. I went into the kitchen to prepare his breakfast, but when I looked around to feed him, he was nowhere to be found. Nowhere! After making sure I hadn't left the door open to the garage, I rechecked all Rockey's favorite haunts: beside the desk in the study, the sofa in the den, his bed under the foyer table. Where had that dog gotten to? I felt my heart rate increase in direct proportion to the speed with which evil scenarios hatched in my head. The only uncharted territory remaining was the second floor, but Rockey didn't climb stairs. With a shrug of desperation, I tiptoed up the stairs in the semi-darkness so as not to wake Prema and Sam. When I reached the top landing, I looked to the right and saw the silhouette of Rockey lying on the floor in the guest bedroom at the far end of the hall. That inner voice with which anyone who reads my books is familiar led me to speak in whispers to Rockey and, for some reason, argued against turning on a light. I continued to talk to Rockey as I crept toward him when all of a sudden, the blankets on the bed moved, and Sam lifted his head and looked at me! Thought I would die! Squeaked out an apology on the fly as I turned and fled back down the stairs hoping that Sam would either not remember the incident, or think I had been part of a bad dream. Whatever Sam thought, he had the grace not to mention it when he came downstairs a couple of hours later and watched some of the Wimbledon tournament with me.

Sam and Prema left for Toronto the following morning for a five-day spiritual sabbatical, thus eliminating the chance for a repeat foray into Sam's bedroom while he slept in it. Lesson learned: Just because an owner says their dog doesn't climb stairs is no guarantee that he never will.

ROCKEY'S SOCKS

The last time I saw Rockey, the pads on his hind paws were red and sore. The cause of the irritation was unclear, but Prema gave me some powder to massage into the pads. And Rockey again had to wear the dreaded cone to prevent him from licking and chewing his feet.

I wanted to ease Rockey's discomfort, so I looked around and found two old socks that I slipped over his feet like booties. The result was a win on all counts. Maybe the softness and warmth of the socks soothed him, and maybe they cushioned his feet against the hard ground. Whatever their effect, Rockey seemed to understand that these makeshift bandages were a good thing, and he accepted them without objection. He could no longer lick the irritated pads, and I didn't see him try to chew or remove the socks. And best of all, he didn't need to be confined by that nasty cone. The socks had no effect upon his ability to walk, although he did look at me with a canine version of an eyeroll at the pink and yellow ribbons I used to tie the booties in place.

I received a text from Prema several months later that Rockey had made his way to Rainbow Bridge. Though I'd known him for one short summer, he had added much love and laughter to my life during that time.

Twenty-four

Later that summer, while caring for Duncan the Corgi again, I thought it'd be fun to take in a local dog park for an impromptu play date with as-yet-unmade friends. I floated the idea past Duncan who agreed to swap his 10:00 walk and manic bubble-chasing time for a new adventure. So I hauled my little canine charge over to a park I'd passed on the way to the gym, only to discover that the one tiny pen was empty of other dogs, but crammed with agility-training structures. Duncan, ever the good sport, made a game (or maybe a mission) of peeing on every single ramp, tire, bench, and leaf at least once. He pooped for good measure in a pile of twigs, and engaged in an altercation of sorts with a garbage can that clanked when he bumped it. Our hero crab-jumped away, growled at it, and gave the offending can a wide birth thereafter. And in response to my laughing at him, he fixed me with a sidelong dirty look that was priceless. All was forgiven and forgotten,

Duncan

however, when I gave him a treat at home and promised him a marathon bubble/frisbee session in the afternoon.

Twenty-five

Nancie, Duncan's owner, buys and flips houses—large beautiful houses, which she either rents or lives in for a couple of years, and then sells. When I've cared for Duncan, I've stayed in a private apartment within one of her houses, or had an entire rental to myself. A resort-like environment for me either way. Then my most recent assignment with Duncan at the time of this writing, my longest assignment, and the first during which I lived in Nancie's actual living space for three and a half weeks while she guided tourists around Australia—just in time for our New Jersey summer's first official heat wave.

And just in time for the town to declare Lake Hopatcong off-limits to swimming and fishing because of widespread harmful bacteria in the water. *Geez!* So I prepared for the assignment with Duncan at his lakefront home not anticipating fun paddling around in the water, but rather standing on the end of the dock and gazing out across the lake…and dreaming.

I awoke at 6:00 the first morning of my assignment, leaned down from the bed to say good morning to Duncan lying on the floor, and walked into the hall where sunlight shining through floor-to-vaulted-roof windows and reflecting off the lake almost blinded me. Staggered across the hall to the bathroom to insert my contacts for a later time when I could open my eyes against the light, and felt my way downstairs clinging to the banister.

Several hours later, Mother Nature wrapped us in easy sunlit warmth that promised to favor whatever adventures embarked upon by Duncan's and my unfettered hearts.

HEATING UP

Three days into my assignment, temperatures rose into the upper eighties and the humidity topped ninety percent. The house with its wall of glass became wicked hot inside. I lowered the Nest thermostat to 68 degrees, and then to 66 degrees, with little effect. I increased the speed of the counterclockwise-rotating ceiling fans to high, which made enough of a difference that Duncan, for a time, no longer lay like an unrisen cake on the cool hardwood floors.

But the temperature and humidity continued to rise with each new day, and the daytime temp in the house increased in direct proportion to Mother Nature's baking spree, despite my turning the thermostat further and further down. At one point, I had the setting at 64 degrees and the ceiling fans rotating on high, but the actual temp on the Nest read 85 degrees. I didn't understand why the air conditioning shut off if the temperature in the house remained above the Nest setting—let alone twenty degrees above the setting! But I learned that if I stood in front of the thermostat, I could "trick" it into turning on. So every couple of hours, I ran upstairs, raised my arms in front of the Nest, and directed all my body heat at the thermostat until it kicked on.

Duncan

MELTING DOWN

About the time the heatwave began, the refrigerator got into the act as well. I had noticed that my milk tasted a little warmer than normal. And when I reached into the ice tray for an ice cube to give to Duncan, the cubes felt wet and had begun to stick to each other. Didn't think too much about it…until the following morning, July 4, when I noticed a lot of water on the kitchen floor outside the side-by-side fridge. I opened the freezer door. The ice cube tray leaked water and contained one large sculpture-like chunk of partially melted cubes. I also saw a once-upon-a-time frozen chicken breast and three gallons of Breyer's French Vanilla soup. A glance at the temperature settings in the fridge explained the problem: "Freezer 42 degrees; refrigerator 54 degrees." Not good! I studied the controls and pushed a button labeled "maximum cool." Encouraged to see the settings readjust to 0 and 37, respectively.

And then I set to work with a roll of paper towels to sop up the water on the kitchen floor. An hour later, the digital readouts in the fridge still read 0 degrees and 37 degrees. But the temps inside felt no cooler, and more water ponded on the floor. When I checked the temps a few hours later, they read 41 and 47. *Vinny!*

The good Wookiee stopped by the house after work, but couldn't find a cause for the rising temperatures inside the fridge and freezer. He did notice, however, that he couldn't hear the compressor engage, and since no refrigerator runs in total silence…

I tried to call Nancie's son, the emergency contact she'd given me, but restrictions on his phone would not allow my call to go through. Kitchen Aid's website provided an equal amount of help.

The idea of texting Nancie that I'd broken her fridge (even though I didn't know how I could have) sat like a greasy ball in my stomach. Could I have messed something up when I lowered the temperature on the Nest? I knew those gadgets could be programmed to control almost an entire house. But I swallowed hard, and detailed the situation in a text to her. Would she like me to set up a service call for the following afternoon? As luck would have it, I needed to be at my own house ten minutes away for a few hours the next morning while a new water conditioner was installed. And I wondered not for the first time why the universe so enjoys blasting potholes before me into which I always tumble.

Nancie's initial response to my text discounted the idea that the Nest controlled the fridge. Either she'd replaced the ice tray incorrectly before she left a few days earlier, or something within the fridge and freezer had prevented the doors from closing all the way. Please toss any and all food that had defrosted. See what happens overnight.

FIREWORKS

Later that evening, I sat with Duncan on Nancie's porch that runs the full length of the house and awaited with mixed emotions the sights and sounds of celebratory Fourth of July fireworks. The porch overlooks the lake and sits high above the shoreline, and thus provided me with a panoramic view of firework displays from several neighboring towns. And with nothing to muffle the sound across the water, I got to hear most of the bangs and several finales in their ear-splitting glory. Impressive. Duncan watched from my lap and barked once or twice, but during the rare moments of explosion-free silence over those couple of hours, I could hear near-constant panicked barking and howling from several other dogs in neighboring houses. I thought about the wildlife that ran terrified from their nests and dens into the streets. And I thought about the veterans who'd returned home from active deployment in the Gulf or some other hell on earth, and relived the horrors of war in their dreams. How frightening for them to hear all those bombs!

IT'S ALL GOOD

When I awoke the following morning, the first thing I noticed was that the house felt cool. I checked the Nest and saw that it had reverted to pre-Stormie-adjusted temperature! And its face said "Nest is on WiFi," which sounded like a good thing to me. I didn't know why or how it had begun working. Just happy it did.

The refrigerator had also returned to normal…after I'd tossed three gallons of melted vanilla ice cream! Oh, how that hurt! All those cream sickle hopefuls washed down the drain.

I again considered the possibilities that the Nest controlled more than just the temperature in the house, and that I had indeed caused the fridge to malfunction when I'd adjusted the thermostat. Compressors don't fail and then regenerate themselves. And I had seen nothing in either the fridge or the freezer to prevent the doors from closing. But if the fridge was connected to WiFi, and WiFi had failed… But WiFi hadn't failed, because I'd never lost Internet access. Had the power gone out? Didn't think so. I would have heard the generator fire up after even a momentary blip of power.

Half a world away, Nancie tried to make sense of what was happening in her house, and insisted that the door to the freezer had to have been ajar. A friend of hers would stop by to evaluate the remaining food in the fridge and freezer. Greg, a computer whiz who builds robots as a hobby, arrived, checked everything, and thought all looked okay. He texted Nancie from her living room while I sat on the opposite sofa, and put her mind at ease. And because he saw nothing on the Nest that implicated me in the malfunction of the fridge and freezer, he put my mind at ease as well.

But I continued to buzz around in bewilderment. Both the thermostat and the freezer/fridge returned to normal over the same night, and that defied all logic if they were not somehow connected. Another unsolved mystery!

WHEN I DIDN'T LISTEN

Midway into the first week, and another hot sticky day on tap. I took Duncan to the dog park early—a larger dog park than the one I'd brought him to the previous summer, and the one to which Nancie brought him on a regular basis—and found it deserted. Duncan, who almost always tries to make the best of any situation, lay at me feet looking pitiful while I played on Facebook in a bit of steamy shade afforded by a small gazebo-type shelter.

Then, without fanfare or any tangible stimulus whatsoever, I decided it was time to leave. Now! This instant! Okay. I reached for Duncan who was thrilled at the prospect of being leashed (a first!), walked out the gate toward the car, and within half a minute, saw three more dogs and their humans approaching us on the walkway. Duncan got happy. I turned around to return to the dog pen so my Corgi for a month could play. And that little voice squawked in my head. Get in your car, it said. Drive, it said. Duncan could play another time, it said. But I ignored said little voice—almost always a mistake. Once inside the enclosure and released, all the dogs had a high old time sniffing each other out and making new best buddies. And I had the unmitigated gall to think to myself that this one time, the voice didn't know what it was talking about. Featherbrained girl!

While the other dog owners and I chatted under the shelter from the sun, one couple mentioned that they'd seen a large black bear crossing the road from the direction I would've driven if I'd left when instructed by that ethereal force to do so. Had I listened to that little voice, there's a good chance I'd have seen my first bear that day!

PROMISED RAIN

The third consecutive melt-me-where-I-stand hot day. And I, despite advancing dark clouds gearing up on the horizon to drench our parched state, spun the wheel of fortune and decided to shuttle

Duncan to the park. I brought one of Duncan's bubble guns with us in anticipation of being the only ones willing to chance the forecasted inclement weather.

But as we walked up the path to the pens, I saw that at least two dozen dogs of all sizes and breeds romped in the large-dog enclosure. The small-dog enclosure jumped with activity as well. Figured I needn't have bothered carrying the bubble gun up the path to the pen.

Wrong! Duncan knew I had it with me. He'd been eyeing it in the car during the entire drive to the park, and he would not be denied once we entered the enclosure. It mattered not to him that his buddies crowded the gate and swarmed around him in welcome when we entered. Or that other dogs attempted to distract him as he chased the bubbles that I released into the air.

Seems the only thing on this good earth that might override Duncan's fixation with bubbles is a squirrel that finds its way into Duncan's sphere of vision. And at best, I'd bet even money on the squirrel over bubbles.

As an aside, Duncan feels obligated to mark every few feet when we walk. Gets a little frustrating for me sometimes. Then one morning, a brainstorm! We trudged home in the humidity-saturated heat, stopping at almost every rock, tree, and mailbox so Duncan could do his macho thing, and I murmured "bubbles." Well! He stopped in mid-sniff of an interesting flower. Head jerked forward. Ears pricked. Legs pumped at hyper-speed. So great was his eagerness to get with bubbles that he pulled me up the final steep hill with the leash extended to near-maximum length. And any time he deviated from the straight and narrow to investigate some smell that might impede our progress, I repeated "bubbles," spurring him on as he threw himself forward into his harness like a plow horse in the fields. He pretty much dragged me down Nancie's driveway in his enthusiasm to reach the backyard bench where he knew the bubble supplies lived.

But so long as the temps flirted with triple digits, it seemed that Duncan was more enamored with the idea of bubbles rather than the physical act of chasing them for long. He let several high-flying bubbles pass him by, which he would almost always track, jump at, and pop with his mouth under more moderate weather conditions.

And I'd discovered a means by which to convert Duncan's and my lethargic stop-and-go walking into a high-powered aerobic session for both of us. Eureka!

Back to the park where ponderous storm clouds all but guaranteed the heatwave's departure. Another Corgi arrived to join the company of small dogs in their respective enclosure, remained for a short while, and left before I could bring Duncan over to meet one of his kin. Duncan, for his part, appeared not to regret the missed opportunity. Too busy trying to impress a pretty Border Collie who was part of the canine assembly in the large-dog pen. I watched him chase her around the field and snap at her heels, and I thought to myself, "He's trying to herd her." Really, Duncan? You want to herd a Border Collie? A breed legendary in its ability to herd? It seems dogs, too, engage in delusions of grandeur!

While the dogs enjoyed their morning play, we humans raised our faces to the sky and spread our arms wide in welcome relief as refreshing breezes ushered in a cold front. Black clouds lingered off to the north and west of us, teased us. Any time now. But none of us moved to retrieve our dogs as blue skies and bright sunshine held court overhead and negated any urgency to break from the comfort of easy fellowship under the canvas canopy at Turkey Brook Park that morning.

The much-anticipated storm arrived around 5:00 in the afternoon. A beauty, but worthless in freeing the mid-Atlantic from the brutal humidity.

MARINE LIFE OF A DIFFERENT SORT

Ping! I heard the notification almost every morning when I turned on my phone. Australia is fourteen hours ahead of the United States, and Nancie would send me texts from the following day that my phone would receive late the night before, and that I would read the morning of the day she'd just experienced. Time differences are a hoot! One morning, her text read, "Bear spotted swimming in lake off Maxim (the street, a long street, where I was staying). She has cubs. Be careful with Duncan." The photo attached to the text made the story real, and it didn't faze me that the photo had been taken eight hours earlier. I ran over to the giant window overlooking the lake to see the bear. Nothing. *Pffft!*

I pulled on shorts and a shirt, leashed Duncan, and headed outside. Had just pulled the front door closed when I thought I saw a cub run across the driveway up by the street. By the time, I'd urged a confused Duncan back inside and jogged up the long path from the house to the garage, and then up the even longer driveway to the road, there was no sign of a bear…any size bear. Maybe I hadn't seen one at all, despite the image of it remaining razor sharp in my mind. The power of suggestion. But even if I had caught sight of a flesh-and-blood Ursa Minor or Ursa Major, it wouldn't count unless I could get close enough to get a picture of it.

Later that day, while down on the dock with Duncan, I saw a little brown furry creature in the lake. I couldn't tell at first if it was swimming or drowning. A brief seesaw debate waged inside my head: to jump or not to jump into the government-proclaimed sullied water after the animal. But then it dove under like it knew what it was doing, and I saw a broad flat tail. About ten seconds later, it reappeared and sent Duncan into delirium. I watched the critter disappear under the water a second time, and again saw the flat tail. A baby beaver in Lake Hopatcong?

MAKING FRIENDS

I'd promised Duncan a visit to the Morris County 4H Fair, and I always try to make good on my promises. So that Friday morning, Vinny and I piled into his van, Corgi in tow, and headed into Chester to check out the animals.

Duncan made friends with the cows and goats, expressed curiosity about the horses, and ignored the chickens and ducks. Then a quick break for some kind of typical fair-type food, ordered for no real purpose other than to sit on a bench out of the sun for a few minutes, and to give Duncan a bowl of water.

With our shirts not quite so drenched with sweat, we wandered over to a tent in front of which stood several large wood carvings of animals. As we approached, Duncan spied a carving of a bear—a most fierce-looking bear indeed in Duncan's mind—and launched into a barking and growling conniption, almost yanking the leash from my hand as he bolted from side to side looking for the best vantage point from which to attack the ursine menace. He observed a wolf and a bobcat carving with polite interest. But when we retraced our steps and passed the bad ol' bear, Duncan resumed his aggressive shenanigans, causing several other fairgoers to stare with momentary alarm or amusement at the little dog gone berserk.

We didn't remain at the fair more than a couple of hours. The sun grew stronger by the minute in the sparsely shaded field, and as we turned toward the parking lot, we saw a gal arriving with her dog. Turns out Fanny was a Corgi-Sheltie mix, and a beautiful girl she was. Duncan thought so, too, and wasted no time ratcheting up his ample charm and striking up a conversation with a kindred spirit.

HEAT OVERLOAD

Nancie's house—this particular house—sits at the bottom of a long driveway that empties onto a forty-mile-an-hour road and a blind curve. A generous shoulder affords competent drivers the means to back onto the street in relative safety. Or, depending upon the size of the vehicle, the driveway itself provides enough room for the less adventurous to execute a K-turn.

I, however, do not like backing into traffic even in a parking lot, and didn't want to deal with making three-point turns in the driveway. And because I don't follow the standard practice of twisting in my seat, bringing my right arm up and across the back of the passenger seat, and looking out the rear window when driving in reverse, I've learned how to use my mirrors. Gotten pretty good at it, too, using my rearview mirror until I cut my wheels, and then relying upon my sideview mirrors to prevent me from driving into immovable objects on either side of me. Confident with my bag of tricks, I opted to use said shoulder to back into and down Nancie's long driveway to the garage while staying with Duncan. A little hairy at first, but after a couple of times, I had the hang of it.

I returned from the gym one morning, pulled onto the shoulder as usual, and began my backward descent into the driveway after using my rearview mirror to watch for possible traffic approaching on the street from behind. Saw in my sideview mirror that the rear bumper of my truck was way too close to the boat parked on the far side of the driveway, so I pulled forward to try again. When I backed up a second time, I looked for the double-wide red brick paving in my sideview mirrors. Where was it? *Geez!* Too close to the boat again! Pushed the stick shift into first gear, released the clutch, and glanced to my right just as I began to roll forward…and saw Nancie's minivan with the "For Sale" sign in the windshield one driveway over. I had tried *twice* to back into the wrong driveway, and a much narrower driveway at that. It never registered with me that Nancie doesn't even own a boat!

Shook it off, maneuvered into the correct driveway, and chalked my temporary lapse of cognitive functioning up to heat-and-humidity-fried brains.

TO SAVE THE WILD THINGS

A friend posted on Facebook a few days later that she and her husband had rescued ten baby possums from the pouch of their mama who had been hit by a car and killed.

And while returning from the gym (again) along the narrow twisty roads in the Hopatcong Heights, I saw another possum lying on the side of the road. My friend's adventure foremost in mind, I found a safe place to pull over and park about half a football field away from the animal. I then donned a clean pair of bright blue surgical gloves that I always carry in my car (because, hey, ya never know!), grabbed Duncan's towel from the front seat, and headed back to the dead possum.

As I walked up the road as close to the guardrail as I could, cars rocketed around curves and passed me in close enough proximity that I could see the occupants' faces—some rolled their eyes, some stared back at me, and some looked concerned like they may have considered stopping if the circumstances in their life or in this world were different. And I thought about the wisdom of risking my life for a possum. I also wondered at the sight I must have presented trudging up the street with my half-in/half-out ponytail, my drenched gym garb, my rubber gloves, my dark glasses, and a large beach towel draped over my arm. Maybe I looked like a character imagined by some deranged horror writer—a character who had descended into madness, and now looked to retrieve the treasured bangles worn by a buried body. These thoughts, coupled with my apprehension of the condition in which I might find the possum, made for an uneasy trek.

But when I reached the animal, I saw with relief, albeit sad relief, that it was a raccoon and not a possum. And it was indeed dead. Had it not been, I'd have wrapped it in the towel, carried it back to my truck, and taken it to my wonderful and compassionate veterinarians, Drs. Hallihan and Casulli, at Animal Care Center in Landing, five minutes away. Wouldn't be the first time I'd brought an injured wild animal to a vet.

GUILTY AS CHARGED

Duncan slunk through the kitchen with his head down and his ears flat back against his skull. He didn't look at me standing behind the island, which I thought odd because he watches everything I do. Didn't even stop to scavenge for crumbs on the floor while I made breakfast for myself. Most peculiar. And then I looked over the island into the living room and saw an obliterated stress ball on the rug. I wasn't sure if it had been in his toy bin, or if he'd filched it from somewhere in the house. But his guilty demeanor hinted strongly at thievery. At next sighting, Duncan lay curled up at the end of the hall in a corner outside the laundry room trying to make himself invisible by melting into the door and the floor. Excellent camouflage on the tan hardwood floor against a white wall. And oh, my goodness, the body language! He refused to make eye contact with me. Just stared trancelike at some imaginary point in space. Think he knew he'd been naughty?

CHANGES

By the middle of the second week, the outside temperature had climbed to 98 degrees, and the humidity made it feel like 115 degrees. Found myself staring more and more often, and for prolonged periods of time at the lake…and at the people taking pleasure in it: the boaters, the water skiers, the jet skiers, the fishermen, all of whom appeared not the least bit concerned by the government's warning of dangerous bacteria in the water.

That water looked *so* good! It didn't appear funky. No green algae covered the surface. We weren't in a cove where township reports claimed the bad algae bloomed. Temptation to walk down to the edge of the dock and jump into the lake tortured me. It played with my head. The algae thing was a hoax, a conspiracy of some kind. But I was afraid to even sit on the edge of the dock and dangle my feet to wiggle my toes in the cool water. Who knew the lack of a bathing suit would be all that stood between caution and the urges of my inner child? I mourned my once-devil-may-care-spirit that had receded at some point along the timeline of my life, and been replaced by a wuss.

Then came the blessed day when Mother Nature wearied of watching us along the mid-Atlantic trudge through life in slow motion, and she laughed and released us from her ruthless heatwave in flamboyant fashion. Dark gloomy clouds hanging low over the lake and appearing to push shoreline trees into the water harbingered what would turn into an all-day spectacular event of continuous thunderstorms and torrential wind-driven rain in New Jersey. Oh, happy day! So many storms lined up along the cold front from the west that they lit up the meteorologists' maps on the Weather Channel like an airport runway.

The deluge came. And then a leaf, a single leaf, blew onto one of the skylights. Duncan noticed it. Of course he did! Nothing gets past that Corgi, and he spazzed out. His frantic gyrations—leaping from armchair to armchair, and running in tight circles beneath the window—accompanied by constant threats and cusses, failed to scare the leaf off the glass. After ten minutes of giving the audacious leaf what for, he retreated with heaving ribs and lolling tongue—but serene aplomb—to the glass wall, where he feigned profound interest in the loss of power on the far side of the lake. Better than admitting to himself that he'd been bested by a leaf!

The aftermath of that wild day of storms? Several days of picture-perfect weather with bright sunshine, balmy temperatures, and low humidity, all compliments of a dry refreshing breeze from the north rather than that hot sticky soup from the southwest.

THE MORNING AFTER

Moments of nothing much happening occur few and far between in my life when I'm playing in the kitchen, driving my car…or pet sitting.

Case in point: While in the shower the morning after the storms, I heard the smoke detector outside the bathroom begin to chirp! *What the…??!!* I expect the alarm to go off when I cook. In fact, a lot of times, Vinny disconnects ours before I have a chance to set a pan on the stove. But Duncan and I were the only living organisms—mobile living organisms—in the house, and I wasn't playing anywhere near a stove.

The only thing I could figure that triggered this alarm was that maybe the battery needed to be replaced. *Hmm.* How to remove the gizmo from the ceiling so I could stop the constant shrill beep beep beep before it drove me nuts? Duncan—he who displayed an athleticism worthy of any Alisted sports star's admiration because he saw a leaf on the skylight—couldn't have cared less about the sudden and constant squawking that would almost certainly do me in if left to continue unabated.

But I saw nothing tall enough on which I could stand to disconnect the smoke detector from the ten-foot-high ceiling in the hall. Not even downstairs, had I for a moment considered an attempt at carrying something up from the first floor.

After I'd stared unblinkingly at the detector for a minute or so and entertained ideas of smashing the thing down with a broomstick, the alarm lapsed into silence of its own accord. I wondered if the steam from the hot-as-I-could-stand-it shower water wafting into the hallway might have set it off. The detector is located just outside the bathroom door, less than five feet from the showerhead. I'd never heard of such a hair-trigger alarm, but the drastic change in outside temperature made the house feel cool, almost damp that morning. Could've confused the smoke detector. I mean, I'd called fuzzy socks into service from my suitcase to keep my feet warm when I'd gotten out of bed an hour earlier!

Bottom line: I'd rather think along the lines of troublemaking steam than imagine yet another mischievous spirit playing games with me.

DEPARTURE

As always when leaving a client's house, I tried to leave Nancie's house pretty much as I'd found it.

It's almost a standing joke between Nancie and me that bubble guns don't fare well when left alone with me. I've broken several in the past. But before leaving for Australia, she showed me the correct way to operate the simple gadget: gentle steady pressure on the trigger to get multiple bubbles, rather than continuous pumping of the mechanism. Ahh, so that's the trick. No wonder I kept killing the tiny spring within the gun. But alas! A bubble gun left outside on the bench during the past three weeks had split at the seam, either from excessive heat or torrential storms. And this caused me no little dismay. Even though the luckless bubble gun didn't join the ranks of damaged from misuse, it had still met its demise on my watch.

In retrospect, July passed in a blink, as do all good times. Had I not kept a journal of sorts detailing my time with Duncan, I would have been hard-pressed to remember being with him at all. It was a fabulous month with all its twists and turns, and it reminded me of how blessed I am to live the life I do: a little crazy, a little nomadic, full of joy and wonder.

Twenty-six

In my interactions with different breeds and temperaments of animals, I have on rare occasions evoked an aggressive response from a critter—sometimes unmerited, other times justified and resulting from my stupidity.

The first unprovoked incident that I can remember occurred during one summer when I was in my early twenties, long before I dreamed of working with animals on a day-to-day basis. My younger sister Kathy and her husband at the time had asked me to babysit their infant daughter for the evening. Tara would be asleep and would in all likelihood remain asleep the few hours I would be there. I could watch the Jets/Patriots football game on television (amazing the details one remembers!) or play with their ginger cat while Tara slept. Easy peasy, right?

Turned out that Pumpkin was neither the most playful nor stable of felines, and suffered from an identity crisis big time. Thought he was a tiger. Took his instinctive responsibility for protecting Tara to the extreme. The first time I went into the bedroom to check on Tara, Pumpkin catapulted from his perch on the living room chair and attacked my shorts-clad legs with a vengeance, drawing blood with several bites and scratches. I spent the remaining evening in dread fear of Pumpkin who glared at me with a baleful countenance, and hissed at regular intervals. And those times when I attempted to reach out to him to let him know that I was one of the good guys, he didn't want to hear it. More hissing. Sometimes, he would think it prudent to jump at me if I so much as moved from the sofa for a drink of water, maybe just to remind me that he was still there and in charge. In self-defense, I wrapped a towel around my bare legs so the well-meaning but schizoid cat could inflict no further damage on my person. And I took to closing Tara's bedroom door behind me every time I went to check on her before the cat could follow me into the room and vent his rage upon my legs. A visit to the hospital emergency room the next day for a tetanus shot set things right. I don't remember if Kathy ever asked me to babysit for Tara again, but Pumpkin and I never shared one-on-one time again.

Another unprovoked episode occurred a decade or so later when I was in the process of selling my beloved Mustang GT convertible. The buyer, Carol, wanting to seal the deal as soon as possible, had brought me to her house so she could hand me her cashier's check rather than waiting for it to be delivered to me by mail. When we entered the house and I saw her dog, one of my soon-to-be-famous premonitions of something bad about to happen flashed through my mind. I was afraid of the dog the minute I saw it—a reaction I'd never before experienced. And the dog, a medium-sized mixed breed, must have sensed my fear because it attacked me and bit my again shorts-clad legs in several places. I was terrified, and Carol was stunned as she hurried to restrain her dog. While I swabbed the gashes with alcohol-soaked gauze, Carol offered to pay any medical bills, but insisted her dog had "Never done that before." The bites, though not serious, were numerous and caused enough bruising to make me look like I'd been bashed with a baseball bat. But one tetanus shot later, and all was good. I never understood my initial knee-jerk reaction to the dog, and I never understood why the dog came at me unless, as often said, it smelled my fear. And I still can't be sure that my premonition wasn't premature and, in fact, generated its own self-fulfilling prophecy.

Then there have been those times when common sense took a back seat to hare-brained lunacy on my part, and resulted in an animal expressing its annoyance—like the time I approached a sweet-looking cocker spaniel that was tethered outside a high-end supermarket. Forget the established protocols for approaching a strange dog: Don't touch. Always ask permission from the owner. Blah, blah, blah. I just had to give the little dog a scritch. The Cocker leaned into my hand with pleasure, but then without warning snarled and snapped at me, maybe because I'd touched a sensitive area behind its ears. While I sustained no injury from the encounter, I was mortified. My embarrassment and surprise, however, were trumped by the sight of two men racing out of the store and across the parking lot to the adjacent train tracks while yelling and pushing a full shopping cart. Seconds later, a woman followed, and screamed for someone to stop the guys who had stolen her cart containing groceries and her handbag. As I remember, there was no one in the parking lot except for me, and by the time I'd recovered from the surprise of the dog's aggressiveness a moment ago and absorbed what I had just seen with the shopping cart, the two thieves were long gone. I could do nothing except express my compassion, and offer the woman a dime for a phone call… and wonder at how such an incident could happen in the tony town of Chatham, New Jersey.

On occasion, I've received minor injury from an animal by sheer accident—exuberance on the part of the animal, as with my squeaky-crazed ferret, Gizmo.

Milano, a pint-sized fur ball, has toys scattered throughout his house. Full of Pomeranian hijinks, he will bring a toy to me, drop it at my feet, and wait for me to throw it so he can chase it, bring it back, drop it again, and let me attempt to pick it up before he grabs it. And if I appear reluctant to play, he'll always give me time to reconsider by sitting in front of me, grinning with anticipation, and nudging the toy closer to me in case I don't see it. After a time, he'll leave, only to return a few moments later with another ball he thinks I might like better.

Those times when all his favorite toys wind up under one of the living room sofas, his growls and frantic digging at the carpet signal that it's time for me to get down on my hands and knees to retrieve them for him. One such time, Milano was on the sofa and got so excited when he saw me drop to fetch his toys that he launched himself at me, and his skull made contact with my face, splitting my lower lip. A quivering mass of energy in the throes of hysteria, he reminded me of a pinball on steroids. To prevent a second "attack," I grabbed him by his scruff with one hand while the other was at my mouth, and put him on the floor. Milano, unhappy with what he perceived as my disrespectful treatment of him, looked at me when released, growled (much as a child might stick out his or her tongue at Mom after sensing the "danger" had passed), and ran off, only to return seconds later with another ball in his mouth for me to throw.

Milano

Twenty-seven

I get to spend at least a week, sometimes two, every May with Mia and Milano, the high-energy Pomeranians, while Teri and Stephen vacation in Aruba. One such assignment began with a bump.

Milano had some diarrhea and then continued to strain without success as if he still felt pressure. This behavior concerned me as thoughts of intestinal blockages slunk unbidden into my head. When Milano's symptoms remained unchanged after two days, and despite no discernible reduction in his natural ebullience or appetite, I called Teri in Aruba. Her matter-of-fact response, "Oh, he probably ate something…like a worm," cracked me up. But she agreed that a phone call to the vet might be a good idea.

I spoke to the veterinary technician who recommended that I feed Milano rice and boiled chicken over the next thirty-six hours. No treats. That last could be a deal-breaker for Milano. But, okay, I'd give it a shot and try to ignore his and Mia's reproachful expressions when treats failed to materialize every time they'd come inside from potty breaks. Teri had rice in her pantry, but no thawed chicken in the fridge. A quick run to Shop Rite remedied that detail.

Milano

By next morning, Milano's poop looked normal. I continued with his rice-and-chicken diet per instructions, and also mixed a little of the people food in Mia's bowl with her normal meals so she didn't feel like Milano was receiving preferential treatment. She didn't know that Milano had an entire bowlful of the yumminess. And Milano didn't seem to care that Mia had a share of his chicken and rice, even though she wasn't sick. Animals are cool that way.

Two mornings after I'd put Milano on the prescribed regimen, I noticed some greenish vomit in one of the dogs' beds. Figured it was grass. Probably from Mia. I caught her lapping up the mess before I could get to it with some wet paper towels, and toss the soiled bedding into the washing machine. And I remembered seeing her grabbing some backyard salad the day before. In addition, she drank half a bowl of water before eating her breakfast—way out of character for Mia with whom food is paramount priority. When she came inside after her early morning surveillance of the yard, she took another long drink. Dehydrated? *Hmm…*I offered her an ice cube on which to chew, but unlike some dogs, Mia gave it a cursory inspection with her nose and walked away from it.

Because neither Mia nor Milano appeared to be feeling sick, I didn't advise Teri of what was going on when we chatted during Teri's routine afternoon phone call to me that day. She and Stephen had renewed their wedding vows the night before, and I wasn't about to con-

Mia

cern them with something else that might turn out to be nothing. I would just keep an eye on both dogs to make sure they didn't eat anymore grass (or worms). They didn't, and all was well...until the night when the rains came and the power shut off.

POWER OUTAGE

The electricity gods were good enough to wait until late evening, just before the dogs went outside for their last potty break, before making everything go kablooey. I located some flashlights, candles, and matches, and let the dogs out on the deck to do their thing in the dark.

After crawling into bed, I called Teri who seemed to think the rain and ensuing power failure were her fault. My sweet funny friend. She added, almost as if trying to mitigate her "guilt," that they had an artesian well. I would have running water. *Hooray!* I'd be able to flush the toilet more than once, unlike when we lost power at our house. *Hooray!* Small luxuries.

And then I called Vinny who, true to his protective Wookiee nature, said he'd be right over with our generator. "No, no, no. It's dark, and it's late, and it's pouring rain. I'll just read in bed by flashlight until I fall asleep. Besides, the power might be restored during the night." Didn't happen. And Vinny, who'd left his phone on all night so I could call him if power was restored, showed up at 5:30 the next morning with our generator and ran a network of extension wires throughout the house so the refrigerator would run, and a lamp or two would operate. AND I could work on my laptop or watch TV, the latter when cable was restored, which turned out not to occur until after restoration of power.

Vinny returned later that day to refill the generator with gas. And the following morning. And yet again later in the day. After one such visit, he said he'd noticed that the main road into the neck of the woods where I was staying was closed off at one fork because of a downed tree. He couldn't see if the tree had taken a power line down with it. Grim visions of superstorm Sandy from a few years back replayed in my mind.

When all was said and done, I endured two and a half days of complete power outage. But how much worse it would have been without Vinny's selfless running back and forth every twelve hours in the rain to minimize my discomfort and hardship!

Against this backdrop of clamminess and near-darkness, Mia and Milano were a pair of troopers and my primary defenses against stir-craziness. Mia cuddled with me as long as I wanted so long as I scritched her behind the ears. And Milano chased and sometimes retrieved balls for as long as I was willing to throw them.

My first full day of power in what seemed like forever (the days kind of all ran together) dawned with bright sunshine, although thunderstorms were predicted for that night. I ventured into the backyard and raised my face to the sky. Rain had spilled from the heavens for seven of eight days in New Jersey. I felt grateful for the lush green foliage, remembering how it hadn't been so long ago that I growled with impatience for spring to knock Old Man Winter down for the count and grace the trees with new leaves. Cabin fever had set in during the recent rains, but I'd developed a kind of mantra to help me cope: "This too shall pass." And when it does, we'll reap the beauty and bounty of a well-watered Earth. Maybe even find some puddles in which to splash while wearing my new flower-patterned Wellies.

Between the sunshine and now-functioning electric lights, I could see well enough to sweep up all sorts of leaves and other debris that had been tracked into the house by wet doggie and human paws. But I noticed with chagrin that a near-infestation of vile dead crickets and one dead centipede had materialized throughout the living room, dining room and foyer under cover of the darkness. You can imagine the effect these discoveries had on me. I ran screaming to the other end of the house where I scavenged for Mia-and-Milano-proof bowls under which to hide the grotesque carcasses so Vinny would have no trouble finding them and dispatching them to where they could do me no harm. But there were so many! A not-so-low-grade horror curdled my gizzard. Had I at any time walked around barefoot during the outage? No, I didn't think so. Gizzard tentatively relaxed.

And then I remembered the powerful ShopVac Teri and Stephen kept in their "green" room or sunroom. Perfect! I lugged it up the stairs and dragged it into the arena of dead creepies, took firm hold of the hose, clenched my teeth, hit "Go," closed my eyes, and swept from side to side. Ten minutes later, this intrepid small human emerged victorious over her dead but fearsome opponents. Mia and Milano accepted the sound and motion of the ShopVac with a ho-hum demeanor while they gathered themselves for a successful launch into ecstatic delirium as soon as they sensed I could turn my attention to them. When my heart rate returned to normal after the ordeal, and the fur babies bounced off the walls in manic delight, I imagined with longing a glass (or several glasses) of Pinot Noir.

The same day I'd vanquished all my adversaries that had been assembled with more than four legs, I had the opportunity to repay Vinny in a small way for his time and effort in helping me live through the power failure. He called to tell me he had locked himself out of the house after having closed the garage door before mowing the lawn, and his remote wouldn't reopen it. Would I please drive over and let him in with my remote? Of course. Twenty minutes later, I pulled into our driveway, uttered a commanding "Open Sesame!" and clicked my remote. The garage door opened without hesitation. A thank you kiss from a thirsty Wookiee, and I returned to Mia and Milano in time to receive a second call from Vinny. Turned out that while he mowed the lawn (almost hearing the grass grow behind him from all the rain we'd received over the past week), a power blip had occurred. Once inside the house, he noticed all the appliance clocks blinking. He had probably tried to reopen the garage door during the five- or ten-minute outage. Timing—it's everything.

Satisfied that all was well, I retreated to Stephen's office with the dogs where I would hunker down for a few hours with the laptop, and Mia and Milano would take some downtime on the carpet behind me or beside me. All was good.

NOT AGAIN!

The following year, I was again with Mia and Milano while Teri and Stephen left for their annual sabbatical to Aruba.

Fell asleep the first night to crashing thunder and frequent flashes of lightning. My kind of weather, despite the accompanying rare and short-lived tornado warning. One resounding boom wakened me to total darkness, and I knew we'd lost power. Two years in a row? You must be kidding! I tossed and turned for about an hour listening for the return of the telltale hum of electricity, and wrestling with the idea of calling Teri to let her know that we were without power again. But what could they do from Aruba? And power might return at any minute. Thought to call Vinny and ask him to stop by and hook up the portable generator for me before he left for work in the morning. Didn't have the heart. Thought about the refrigerator full of steaks, chicken, yogurt, and half-gallon of milk that Teri had bought for me before she left so her pet sitter wouldn't keel over from hunger. Thought about the tangerine Outshine popsicles in the freezer. Thought about having no laptop or television or hot tub. Thought about having no air conditioning if the temps and humidity climbed as forecasted. Thought about all the dampness-loving bugs that would materialize (as they had the previous year). Thought again about calling Vinny, but fell into an uneasy sleep until I awoke at 4:30. The storms had moved on, but the house remained black as pitch. And memories of all the bad things that had occurred during the power outage the previous year returned with crystal clarity. That tied it, and I reached for my cell to call Vinny. *Wait!* This house was always dark at night—the way I like it. In fact, I unplug all the night lights to achieve the darkest dark. Try the lamp beside the bed whispered the voice of common sense. I did so. And there was light! Power had never gone out! Somewhere in that fuzzy state of consciousness between dreaming and fully awake with the storm happening around me…

AND I may have been predisposed to the idea of a power outage, compliments of a friend who had posted on Facebook hours before I went to bed that her cable had gone out at exactly 9:00—just when the *Game of Thrones* finale was about to begin. Oh, the angst!

Twenty-eight

The challenge and joy of caring for a pair of Jack Russell terriers—that breed of dog bordering on mythical in its intelligence.

Finnigan and Pearl live in a large house surrounded by several acres of invisible-fence-contained fields in which the dogs can chase squirrels and any other wild critters bold enough to venture within sight or scent of these dogs. If split personality existed among our canine friends, Jack Russells would be the poster dogs for the psychological disorder: loving and sweet lap dogs when indoors, fierce tenacious predators when outside.

Finn and Pearl sleep in their crates at night. Come morning, they wait in quiet but quivering anticipation for me to release them, fasten their special collars, and punch the automatic garage door opener so they can leap down the two steps into the garage and drop to their bellies to wriggle under the garage door as it continues to rise. Like wound-to-the-max springs released from a can, the dogs streak across the lawn in unmistakable joy...and head straight into the fractured head games of the resident squirrels.

Apparent candidates for suicide by Jack Russell, said squirrels bait Finn and Pearl without mercy (or discernible prudence) on a regular basis. In disbelief, I've watched the thrill-seeking rodents venture down the tree trunks for what appears to be no other reason than to taunt the dogs. The squirrels descend to within inches of the dogs' snapping jaws…and then remain there while Finn and Pearl wear themselves into helpless exhaustion from leaping at their tormentors. Every time! They mock, these squirrels do, as our canine heroes race headlong into the ambush. Every day!

Finnigan and Pearl

Finnigan

Pearl obsesses over chipmunks, perhaps a mental health exercise to distract herself from the harrowing relentless abuse she suffers from the twisted minds of squirrels. No reasonable doubt exists in Pearl's head that chipmunks hang out in the undercarriages of cars—perhaps because she's caught and killed one or more in the past (a fact I neither want nor need con-

Pearl

firmed), and she spends much time and energy underneath any and all cars within the boundaries imposed by the electric fence. With an assiduousness that rivals the most OCD-possessed perfectionist, she stands on her hind legs and inspects every nook and cranny of car chassis in her quest for the mini-rodents. My past concern when I saw her paw at something under my truck was that she would disengage or maybe chew through some essential working of my truck, as she once chewed through the hose that attached to the rear window washer of her human's car. No worries any longer. The electric fence has since been modified to Pearl-proof cars inside and outside the garage.

Mealtimes with Finnigan and Pearl present a challenge, as well as laughter. While Pearl gobbles her kibble in normal doggie fashion, Finn savors one piece at a time—in part because he's a finicky eater by nature, and in part because most of his front teeth are missing. The usual routine plays out with Pearl emptying her bowl in the mud room within seconds, and then walking into the kitchen to sit a few feet from Finn's head to engage in what can only be described as begging. Finn obliges the little girl by placing occasional pieces of his own kibble on the floor beside him for Pearl to snap up.

When walking Pearl and Finn, or to be more precise, when they walk me pulling their leashes taut with disproportionate strength and speed, it's all I can do to keep up with them. The mile-long loop through the upscale neighborhood provides a power walk that vanquishes any guilt I might feel about not making it to the gym for an aerobic workout while visiting my two favorite Jack Russells.

Finnigan

Twenty-nine

I consider myself fortunate to enjoy good physical health for a vintage lady. My biggest and most frequent complaints are those of unholy cluster headaches and their associated remedies! Between the two, they render me close to brainless. They do.

THE TROUBLE WITH HEADACHES

One incident in particular comes to mind. I had taken a Fiorinal and a muscle relaxant to combat brutal spasms that made me feel nauseated and ready to cancel an assignment scheduled to begin later that afternoon. The drugs did their thing, and I realized that fabulous sense of relief that comes when the hammer stops pounding in my head. But my short-term memory had been impaired enough by the time I arrived in Montville, a forty-minute ride from my house, that despite Phil and Debbie commenting on how they were looking forward to hiking in the Scottish Highlands, I said something soon after our conversation to the effect of, "So you're off to see Lady Gaga in Vegas" (their getaway for which I'd been scheduled to pet sit the following February). It's a wonder these amazing clients didn't cancel their flights right then, or make spontaneous alternate arrangements for their animals.

And then, Phil informed me that both his cats, Gene and Fred, had developed thyroid problems. Each cat received one pill in a pill pocket twice a day. But I in my post-headache fog forgot Phil telling me that the kitties had had their full dosage of medicine a little early that day. So while feeding Gene and Fred their treats later that evening, I gave them each another dose. When Debbie phoned from the airport before taking off for Scotland, I told her (well-pleased with myself) that I'd given the cats their thyroid medication without problem, and was mortified to learn that I shouldn't have done so. No need to call the vet, she assured me in response to my question. Just skip their morning dose.

After a guilt-ridden night followed by what had to have been an uneasy sleep, I awoke the next morning to find Gene and Fred running around and meowing with zeal as usual when I got up to feed them (sans pill). The resilience of animals, despite the occasional stupidity of the human who cares for them while Mom and Dad are away, continues to amaze me. Okay. Enough beating myself up over this. I know I'm a competent and reliable pet sitter, but it bothers me that headaches sometimes get me in their clutches.

AGING DOGGIES

In the six months or so since I had last visited Montville, Buddy the happy-go-lucky Borzoi, had been prescribed Cosequin for joint stiffness. Keno the border collie mix, had been taking the medication for at least a year. Both dogs now take a smashed-with-a-meat-mallet tablet mixed in with their breakfast, and I noticed the first morning of my assignment that Buddy left one piece of Cosequin in his bowl. It took two cheese pockets before he swallowed that piece as well. If he were human, I'm pretty sure he'd be one who licked the Oreo center clean and left the cookie.

As they've aged, both dogs have increased difficulty getting into the hatch of my Xterra to be driven to the dog park. Vertically challenged as I am, standing short at a scant sixty-one inches, I bought the truck with the goal of wanting to sit as high as possible, within reason, to increase my ability to see around moving objects ahead of me. Larger tires and stiffer suspension make my vehicle more than three inches higher than Debbie's SUV. The first morning we prepared to visit the park, both dogs jumped in with little hesitation. But much to my alarm, when it came time to leave the park, Keno wouldn't even attempt to jump into the truck. Just stood with his front paws on the hatch and a facial expression that pleaded, "I can't do this. Help me." Counting my lucky stars that it was Keno, the smaller of the two dogs that needed assistance, I boosted his butt into the hatch, and away we went.

Once home, I texted Debbie and asked for her input. She told me Keno wouldn't go near a ramp that she'd bought for him, but suggested I try an old ottoman which the dogs might use as a "step stool" into the hatch. Before undertaking the task of hauling the ottoman out to the car, I thought I'd try the ramp anyway. Keno put two paws on the ramp that I'd placed against the back of my truck, felt it flex under his weight, and wanted no part of it despite my holding a cookie at the top to entice him. Buddy wouldn't even look at the ramp. Point made.

The following morning, I brought the ottoman downstairs and positioned it behind my truck. And then I brought the dogs to the setup for their approval. Keno jumped from the ottoman to the hatch without hesitation—maybe because he saw the cookie I held in my hand. Buddy followed suit. Well worth the minor hassle of lugging the awkward ottoman into the elevator and out through the garage. With Keno and Buddy contained, I hoisted the ottoman into the hatch with the dogs; it was too hard for me to wedge it onto the back seat. A little crowded back there, but a biscuit in exchange for tight quarters during a scant ten-minute ride seemed a fair trade to the dogs. And neither of the boys appeared uncomfortable or stressed by the close quarters.

Almost always the most senior citizens in the dog park, Buddy and Keno turn heads on a regular basis. No one believes me when I say they're thirteen and fourteen years old, respectively. Daily exercise and a sensible diet go a long way toward maintaining spirit, looks, and good health!

In addition to his visible joint stiffness, I noticed other changes in Buddy as well. Sometimes while relaxing in his bed in front of the fireplace, he would drop his head, open his mouth wide as if he wanted to be sick, and emit a horrible sound—kind of a cross between a roar and a gag. Think cheetah coughing up a hairball. *Ack!*

Buddy

And his front paws looked red and raw, either because of or in spite of his near-constant licking them. Debbie suggested I try giving Buddy a larger dose of Cosequin, the same as Keno received.

Then something weird occurred that I would consider pure coincidence if I, in fact, believed in coincidence. For two consecutive days, Buddy neither "gagged" nor licked his paws, and guess what? The angry redness in his paws faded. But during late afternoon of the second day and into the evening, Buddy resumed his licking and "gagging," and the angry color returned to his paws. The indisputable common factor here is that during the two days when Buddy was asymptomatic, the humidity had dropped way down to comfortable levels. His symptoms reappeared with the rise in humidity.

Remembering Rockey's reddened paws, I wondered if Buddy might suffer from some kind of weather-related allergy. And I thought about dealing with his symptoms in the same way I'd dealt with those

Rockey experienced: protect his paws with a couple of old socks. But I could find nothing in the Montville house that looked like a reasonable fix. Following Debbie's advice, I increased Buddy's dosage of Cosequin to the same level as that which Keno took.

During one early morning walk of what turned out to be the first day that Buddy didn't lick his paws, and under clear skies in comfortable humidity and temps, I enjoyed watching the dogs reach out with spring in their step while I lengthened my stride to keep up with them. The sidewalk ends a few feet beyond the Loop and where the road becomes a main drag. I always walked in the street close to the curb while I kept the dogs to my left and on the grass. We crossed the main street as usual when we reversed direction about half a mile down the road and past the cornfields to head home so I could continue to keep the dogs on my left without my having to walk in fields mined with well-camouflaged gopher holes that I sometimes saw ahead of time, and sometimes didn't.

But when we began to re-cross to where sidewalks again existed, Buddy thought it a grand idea to stretch out on his belly in the middle of the street and soak in the warmth of the solar-heated macadam. With rush hour approaching and traffic building, his decision lacked all requisite criteria for being hatched by one of sound mind and body. This was crazy, even for the comedic Buddy. After ascertaining that no physical reason existed for his kooky choice of locations in which to catch some rays, I had to impose my will upon him to get up and walk with Keno and me across the street. Buddy, a large dog, resisted the entire way, walking sideways and refusing to fully straighten his legs until we reached the other side. (Reminded me of Flame, the horse I'd owned years before, who more than once tried to roll with me on his back in midstream.) I, with the dogs in tow, made it across the street without managing to annoy any drivers who were in a hurry to get to work or wherever else people hurry to at 7:00 in the morning…although we may have attracted some amused stares. Buddy's behavior returned to normal once we gained the sidewalk, and we completed our walk without further incident. I came away from the "adventure" baffled by Buddy's behavior, but happy that he was not so large as to prevent me from urging/coercing him out of the street. Love that boy, idiosyncrasies and all.

Along with his other ailments, Buddy's eyesight seemed to be deteriorating at an alarming rate. He tripped over Keno a couple of times when Keno was sleeping on the living room floor. In response to Buddy's diminishing ability to see, I began taking the dogs downstairs in the elevator and through the garage when we went out, rather than walking them down the steep steps outside. I feared for Buddy's safety, as well as my own because of the way he didn't appear to see the steps. He knew they were there, but he just kind of reached out blindly with his paws and half-stumbled/half-fell down the steps. Last time I'd been with him, he'd managed okay if I kept him on a very short leash, stopped him before the steps, and said "down" at each step. Ascending the stairs had seemed easier for him, but I had still kept him on a short leash, stopped him before each group of steps, and said "up."

But now, he seemed to have difficulty even seeing the ottoman I'd placed behind the hatch of the truck. He jumped onto it only when he felt it against his chest, and hesitated to take the step into the truck from the ottoman without strong encouragement from Keno (who almost always leaped in first) and me. When dismounting from the hatch, I had to hold him by the leash loop located close to his collar because he leapt out and sometimes missed the ottoman altogether, once or twice landing hard enough that his rear legs buckled under him. It broke my heart to watch Buddy struggle as his sight continued to decline.

Despite time's relentless pillaging of the animals' physical bodies, I had no trouble getting any of the critters to take all required medications. Thyroid pills offered to and accepted by Gene and Fred twice a day, every day. Heart worm pills offered to and accepted by Keno and Buddy on specified days. Large-dose Cosequin offered to and accepted by both dogs at breakfast. Phenobarbital given to Keno twice a day.

In short, the local home-grown animal apothecary in Montville was open for business and doing well.

A SHAKY PEACE

But that elevator! Before I'd begun using it to transport Buddy and Keno downstairs, I'd cared for the Montville animals many times over a span of four years. And I'd managed to avoid venturing inside the intimidating box until a knee injury hampered my ability to navigate stairs. The elevator was a last resort. After one or two rides in the car, I wondered why I'd allowed my fear of small enclosed spaces to scare me out of using it. I thought of all the times I'd hauled bags of groceries upstairs from the garage and negotiated the keep-the-doggies-separate-from-the-kitties-gate at the top landing while said doggies nuzzled the bags and pushed against me with enough enthusiasm to almost send me back to the basement the hard way. Never again!

I also figured out that it was easier to take the recycling bins down in the elevator and out through the garage rather than assuming the risk of dumping everything, including myself, down the outside brick steps. On one such recycling trip, I entered the elevator, closed the door, and hit "1" to take me downstairs. Nothing! *Hmm*. A second attempt yielded the same non-response. Rolled my eyes, blew air through closed lips in frustration, and opened the elevator door. Correction. In a perfect world, I would have opened the elevator door. But in this imperfect fallen world, the door remained locked! I couldn't get out, and the elevator wouldn't move. Claustrophobia hit hard in the next picosecond. When my heartbeat slowed to something akin to the speed of a blender on low, I reached for my cell to call Vinny. And then I saw it! Not a cave cricket or a centipede. Thank you, God. Rather, I saw that I hadn't pulled the gate closed. More air through closed lips, this time in relief as I pulled the gate to, hit "1" again, and felt the car begin to move. Once downstairs, I slid the gate to the left, opened the elevator door, carried the recycle bin out through to garage to the curb, reentered the house, and climbed the stairs back to my laptop where I hoped to wax creative.

But all I could think as I stared at the computer screen was *what if*? What if there had been a creepy, eight-or more-legged creature in that elevator with me when I couldn't get out?

HOMEWARD BOUND

A few days later at the park, Buddy and Keno met up with Simba, a Shiba Inu, and made friends with another small dog who got Keno running, even in the miserable August heat. While the dogs' respective humans sprawled on benches in what little shade the few saplings in the park provided, I noticed a tiny creature crawling across the hot gravel. Thinking it was a frog, I moved in for a closer look and saw instead a baby snapper no bigger than the little green turtles found in pet stores.

Being the neurotic savior of all creatures that don't scare me—I move worms by the handful from the street after a rain—I wanted to get the turtle off the hot gravel and out of the way of dogs and people who might trample it. I picked it up by its shell, and was amazed at the strength in its tiny legs as it paddled the air with desperate ferocity. When the others saw what I held, one man fetched the park-provided water bowl from the far side of the enclosure. I placed the turtle in the water, thinking that it would swim. It didn't. After I'd tipped most of the water out allowing the turtle to walk around and cool off, I headed for the exit gate with my newest "charge."

There had to be a stream or a pond nearby to which the turtle's instinct had been guiding it before I derailed its forward progress. But I saw nothing except fields outside the enclosure, and some woods a little further out. The other two dog owners agreed to watch Buddy and Keno for a few minutes while I scoped out the immediate area for some natural source of water. As I walked toward the fields, a car pulled into a corporate parking lot adjacent to the park. I headed to the lot and asked the driver if he knew of any stream or pond nearby. "Yes, just into those woods over there. You can see it from here." I walked toward the woods and saw an algae-filled pond about fifteen feet into the woods. Perfect habitat for a turtle.

A step or two into the woods with the turtle when I looked down and saw legions of healthy poison ivy. My crops and anklet socks would provide little if any protection from the menacing plants to which I am sensitive to a ridiculous level, so I removed the turtle from the bowl, placed it as far into the trees as I could reach, watched it head toward the water, and trusted Mother Nature to get it there in safety. Happy trails, little one.

COSMIC KARMA

On the day Debbie and Phil were to return from Scotland, I took Buddy and Keno for their usual morning walk. Thunderheads threatened imminent rain, and less than half an hour after we'd arrived back home and gotten inside, the skies opened up with a short but spectacular thunderstorm. *Phew!* No muddy pawprints to wipe from the floor.

But I know better than to assume complacency when cosmic forces appear to favor me. Experience has taught me that the universe has a wicked sense of humor, and doesn't often let me get away with things without some kind of quasi-karmic repercussions—its way of preventing me from becoming smug, I guess. And this dodging-the-deluge event would prove no different.

To set the scene, I'd put together what I'd hoped would be a refreshing beet-and-orange salad the previous night for Debbie and Phil's return home. The following morning, the morning I breathed a sigh of relief for winning the race against rain, I opened the refrigerator to retrieve the dogs' moist food. Aforesaid salad catapulted from its shelf onto the floor. Thank goodness for unbreakable plastic mixing bowls! But the plastic wrap with which the salad container was covered gave way to the force of the heavy beets that slammed against it, leaving one meager serving remaining in the bowl...and a colossal mess splattering at least a three-foot area of the kitchen floor!

Praise the Lord for uncarpeted hardwood floors and easy-to-clean white cabinets, as well as for two patient dogs who made no attempt (after an initial cursory sniff) to hinder the clean-up of what looked like a crime scene. Truth be known, I think they enjoyed watching me on my hands and knees (and listening to me mutter colorful expressions of frustration) while they had a fun chat in doggie speak about the yutz with whom their humans had entrusted them.

Thirty

I returned to Montville the following winter, and Debbie and Phil headed out to Vegas to see Lady Gaga. They really did this time!

Keno, whom I believe holds the never-to-be-equaled-or-challenged record for quantity of disemboweled squeaky toys showed signs of retiring from the games when he showed off his new squeaky in the likeness of Lamb Chop, the sock puppet given voice by the late great Shari Lewis. Throughout the entire time I stayed at the house, Lamb Chop remained intact—the one and only squeaky toy Keno didn't destroy with gusto. To the contrary, he appeared to protect it—cradled it in his paws, licked it. Cuddled with it most of the day.

The young critters and the elderly ones each hold a special place in my heart. But Keno! How he makes me laugh!

Perhaps it's the border collie intelligence in his DNA, but Keno proved himself a shoe-in for the annual PATSY Award when at the park one morning. I released him and Buddy into the enclosure and watched both dogs wander around at a snail's pace…until Roman, an energetic young Rhodesian Ridgeback arrived. The years seemed to fall away from Keno as he ran (with no obvious sign of arthritic hips) to greet the new arrival, and engaged in half an hour of roughhousing with Roman. Poor Buddy, ever the good sport, tried to join in the fun but couldn't always see when Roman charged him. After a few hard bumps and near-knockdowns, Buddy had had enough and wandered over to me for a reassuring pat and safer grounds.

Keno

When the time came for us to leave, Roman's owner contained him while I called "my" dogs to me. Buddy responded to the sound of my voice at once and trotted over to where I stood by the gate. Keno, however, went into his invalid routine and shuffled over to me with his nose inches from the gravel, looking for all the world that life was just too hard. And then, when we arrived at my truck with the trusty ottoman in place, Keno placed his front paws on the ottoman and gazed at me with the most pathetic look I've ever seen. I backed him away, and guided Buddy onto the ottoman and into the truck with no problem. Rewarded him with the requisite biscuit. Keno, upon seeing Buddy receive a cookie, rediscovered his youthful vigor in an instant, and joined Buddy in the hatch without assistance or encouragement from me.

Meanwhile on the home front, Fred, one of the two kitties, refused to eat the new food blend advised by the veterinarian. The cat exhibited all outward signs of being hungry but refused to eat, and had lost considerable weight as a result. Reminded me of Widget and Bella, two of my gone-but-not-forgotten ferrets, who had almost starved themselves to death, despite wanting to eat. When I advised Debbie of what was happening with Fred, she requested that I go to Petco and buy the food she had fed the cats in the past.

So I made an emergency run of sorts to Parsippany Petco, a store to which I'd never been. My GPS got me to the large strip mall in which Petco was located, but I'm here to tell you that whatever Einsteinian engineer designed the entrances and exits to said mall had to have been into drugs! Big time! From fifty miles per hour on route 46, you turn into a one-way, single-lane, curb-bordered chute that zigs and zags until it dumps you into the parking lot proper in front of the stores where a web of scaffolding runs the length of the mall—or did when I was there. And when it's time to leave the mall—well, exiting the parking lot with cat food in tow made my entrance into the lot seem like a walk in the park. Even my GPS convulsed in its disorientation. "Turn right on alley," it chirped. And "In fifteen feet, turn left on alley." Then "In ten feet, turn right on alley." While the GPS recalculated for the umpteenth time, and cars entered and exited and crossed in front of me, I felt like an uninitiated lab rat in a maze with no hope of finding the cheese—or in my case, the exit from a reasonable facsimile of J.K. Rowling's bewitched maze in *Goblet of Fire*. My knuckles whitened as I clenched the steering wheel in a near-death grip. I could feel the knots in my neck and shoulders approach Gordian proportions as, ironically, The Eagles' "Hotel California" played on my radio. Perfect! I checked out of Petco when I wanted. But while I searched for a way out of the serpentine complex, I wondered if I could ever leave. Half an hour (or maybe it was only ten minutes) of attempting to navigate the blasted labyrinth, avoiding numerous too-close-for-comfort encounters with other vehicles, and counting my blessings that at least it wasn't Black Friday, I found the highway again. A euphoric wave of relief as what-amounted-to-a-giant-concrete-and-macadam pinball machine shrunk and disappeared in my rear-view mirror.

When I returned home to four sympathetic fur babies, I googled Walmart. They carry the same cat food. They have a store located less than ten minutes away. And they have a parking lot that doesn't render a person fit for a psychiatrist's couch!

Thirty-one

Thirty-five years—a long time to devote to and study ferrets. Time well spent. And I owned fifteen of the critters, each unique unto itself.

Pokey, a chocolate-colored ferret, was my biter. My aggressive biter. My biter without due cause. No love nibbles from that little miscreant. I sometimes thought I'd received two ferrets for the price of one after I'd brought him home. Good Pokey. Bad Pokey. He'd be stretched out in my arms relaxed and happy, maybe even doling out ferret kisses, and without warning open his little mouth and sink his teeth into me. *Chomp!* But he never drew blood—unlike Gizmo, a ferret I would own years later, who could become so riveted, so zonked-out mesmerized by a squeaky toy when playing that he would jump for it in a blind frenzy and every so often miss, hooking a chunk of human instead. But where Gizmo's bites were accidental and therefore forgiv-

Pokey

able, Pokey's surprise attacks precluded any possibility of unconditional trust I might have developed in him. It got to the point that whenever he began giving me ferret kisses, I'd either set him down on the floor or grab a towel to wrap around my arm.

And when a ferret bites, it doesn't release its "prey" but hangs on and sometimes worries it like a dog might worry a favorite toy. The worst thing a person can do when caught within the jaws of a ferret is attempt to pull away. Instead, said "victim" should fight the knee-jerk reaction to get away from the ferret, and hold still until the animal decides to release him/her.

While one of my smartest ferrets, Pokey behaved one time as if he had no brains at all. He bit an attorney, a friend of mine whom I had invited to my apartment for dinner. Imagine my horror that evening when I emerged from the kitchen into the living room and saw Paul sitting on the sofa with his hand dangling near the carpet, and Pokey attached to one of his fingers! By happy chance, Paul was either too surprised by Pokey's "attack," or smart enough not to resist the ferret. No damage done, although Paul warned me in what I'm certain was only half-jest that if he started running in circles and frothing at the mouth, I might have legal problems.

Ferrets climb, and every one of mine could scale the outside of their triple-decker cage with ease. But upon achieving the summit and checking out the view from on high, they would either attempt to jump off the cage or climb down head first—both dangerous propositions, because their hind legs could catch within the metal latticework of the cage. A scream (and ferrets do scream when frightened or in pain) would bring me running to the ferret's rescue. Pokey alone figured out how to back up to the edge of the cage and climb down the outside, hind end first.

Because they get bored and lonesome without a cage mate, I always owned at least two ferrets at a time. Tango, a silver mitt (gray with white paws), was Pokey's buddy for almost six years and joined Pokey atop the ferret bell curve. But my Tango had no shame. One time,

Tango

after investigating the bathroom waste basket, she hurtled into the living room with a panty liner dangling from her mouth. Rachel, a vet tech friend with whom I'd been chatting on the sofa, dissolved into giggles and turned what could have been one of those moments when I wanted to crawl into a hole and pull the earth over me into a "Ya gotta laugh" situation.

During the time Pokey and Tango lived with me, I bought a Rottweiler-Lab puppy who didn't know quite what to make of the small animals that careened around, turned on a dime, and laughed at the dog with four huge left feet. The desire to play appeared mutual among all parties, but the ferrets were fast enough and smart enough to stay out of harm's way when the exuberant but not-yet-grown-into-her-paws Dakota galumphed after them in games of chase.

To further entertain Pokey and Tango, I'd bought a hollow plastic yellow ball about ten inches in diameter and bored with several ferret-size holes. Dakota wanted to engage with the ferrets when they were inside the ball and running in one hole and out another. On one occasion when Tango escaped the Dakota juggernaut by diving into the ball, the twenty-pound floppy-eared puppy attempted to follow her and succeeded in getting the ball stuck on her snout. Tango, having exited through another hole in the ball, watched in unsuppressed delight as Dakota ran from pillar to post in confusion before knocking the ball from her nose.

Dakota and Boo

When the time came for me to release Tango from this world, Pokey was eight years old. Cataracts clouded both his eyes, and a growth about the size of a pea had developed on his head. But he appeared to be in no distress, and I couldn't bring myself to put him down with Tango.

Instead, I bought a light-colored sable ferret I saw in a pet store window one lunch hour. He was the cutest little thing, so young that his nose was still kind of flat and round. It hadn't developed into the sharp point characteristic of that in more mature ferrets. Impulse, as I named him, captured the hearts of all my AT&T colleagues when I returned to the office with him in a cardboard box. I think it's safe to say that Impulse caused a noticeable productivity dip during the remainder of that Friday afternoon as a near-constant stream of visitors to my cubicle wanted to see the tiny fur baby.

When I took Impulse for a vet check the next day, I learned the ferret was maybe six or seven weeks old; most ferrets are at least ten or twelve weeks old before being sold. The vet put Impulse on a special diet and suggested I keep him in a separate cage (which I'd already done since bringing him home the night before) for at least a month. I don't remember what kind of food I received from the vet, but Impulse ballooned into one of the largest ferret babies I'd ever seen—and in short order, too!

Pokey's and Impulse's cages sat side by side, so each ferret knew he was not alone in the house. Given Impulse's size and Pokey's apparent depression over missing Tango, I placed the baby in Pokey's cage a week earlier than recommended by the vet. But Pokey, despite his blindness, attacked Impulse with such ferocity that Impulse screamed in terror. I returned the "little one" to his own cage, and realized I had to give Pokey more time to grieve the loss of Tango.

But time wasn't the answer. Pokey refused to accept Impulse after several days, even when both were outside their cages. He would sniff out the terrified baby and make a run at him with the clear intention of doing harm. I'd never witnessed nor heard of a ferret-ordained blitzkrieg the likes of which Pokey mobilized against Impulse. Maybe he blamed Impulse for the disappearance of Tango. Maybe he'd been alone just long enough to feel there wasn't room in the house for another ferret. Whatever Pokey's thought processes, I made the difficult decision to return Impulse to the pet store, believing that while he was large, he was only about three months old, had a face to melt the hardest heart, and a personality sweet enough to almost guarantee that he'd find a permanent home soon.

Sometime later, I entered one of those shopping mall pet stores for no reason other than to look at the puppies, and saw an adult dark sable ferret in a cage behind the glass. The poor thing! Surrounded by all the barking dogs, the ferret had to have been frazzled. I bought the creature on sight, and brought him home to meet Pokey who, again, would have none of it. So I kept Boo in the second cage, and bought another ferret to live with him.

Harley was a beautiful ferret, almost white but with dark eyes. I think Boo was so happy to have one of his own kind in the cage with him who didn't want to kill him that he didn't even engage in typical "dominance" play with the baby Harley. They became instant pals.

I found in Harley a kindred Sunday-afternoon football fan. She appeared to favor the San Francisco 49ers as did I, and would sit on the floor in front of the television craning her neck to watch Joe Montana work his magic up and down the gridiron. While I never shared my ever-present bowl of buttered popcorn with her, I did once let her lick

Harley

a drop of Bailey's Irish Cream from my finger. *"Yum!"* if she could speak. Boo, a more conventional ferret, displayed interest in neither football nor liquor. He preferred the simple pleasure of cuddling on my lap.

When Pokey began to show signs of slowing down and feeling sick after his ninth birthday, I made the decision to put him down. He had lived longer than any ferret I had owned to that point, or ever would own. And he now rests forever next to his friend Tango among the irises in the backyard of my Chester cottage.

After Harley and Boo also made their way to Rainbow Bridge, I bought Shasta, another cream-colored ferret baby. She was the last one in the large pet store from where I bought most of my ferrets, so I special-ordered another one from a local private pet store that didn't carry them as a rule. "Too much trouble," in the words of the shop owner. Enter Riblet. He with the gorgeous tail and phenomenal thick dark sable coat.

Riblet

Riblet turned out to be another athletic ferret who topped the bell curve, and one with whom I could play a form of hide and seek during his out-of-cage playtime. He'd count to three while I ran and hid, and then come looking for me. As soon as he'd found me, he'd take off and wait for me to find him, most often behind a living room chair or under the sofa. And then it was my turn to hide again.

Shasta

Riblet and Shasta's favorite toys were small rubber gumball-size doodads covered with nodules—reminiscent of that free-floating mechanism employed by Yoda when disciplining a blindfolded Luke Skywalker to trust The Force. But the ferrets, knowing nothing of the *Star Wars* saga, wanted only a game of chase, retrieve, and stash. Each ferret had its preferred hiding place for treasures, which made it easy for me to collect the half-dozen or so toys I kept aside for playing outside the cage. Riblet most often took his prizes behind one of the two living room sofas. Shasta stockpiled everything she could find under the dining room credenza, after which she enhanced her inventory with playthings from the cage.

To entertain myself and to challenge my "gifted" Riblet, I devised an advanced version of the "chase" game. Rather than throwing the ball for him, I'd place it on a shelf or a piece of furniture when he wasn't looking. And then I'd call him (and he would come when called) and point in the general direction of where I'd "hidden" it—or not. Riblet would follow the direction of my finger and either see the ball and climb or jump to where he could get at it, or return to me with a look of utmost ferret annoyance after he'd realized I'd tricked him and sent him on a wild goose chase.

A brief etymology lesson: "Ferret" from Latin *fur*, "thief." All ferrets "steal" things. It's what ferrets do. Part of their DNA. And nothing is off limits. A paperclip contains as much intrinsic value to a ferret as a beach towel, a stuffed toy, or a diamond ring. What the ferret sees, wants, and can dig out and carry or drag to a secret place…well, ferrets subscribe to the principle that possession is nine-tenths of the law.

Ferrets also love to tunnel through and under snow, dirt, clothes, sofa cushions, whatever. And every ferret I owned found it impossible to resist exploring the legs of empty-of-human jeans that lay within its reach. One time when the ferrets were out of their cage, he/she whose name shall remain anonymous (because I don't remember which one it was, and because I don't want to besmirch the good name of the "innocent" others) showed itself to be the Clyde Barrow of the ferret set. All was quiet—a sure sign of trouble. And then Vinny happened to look up from whatever he was doing just in time to see all his paper money disappearing behind the bedroom bureau. One of my sticky-pawed furry varmints had dug it out from a pocket in a pair of jeans that were lying on the floor. Had Vinny noticed his money missing without seeing the burglary in progress, he'd have right away figured a ferret took it, and embarked on a search of all known hiding places—and maybe some unknown and creative ones (like when I found my keys in the broiler drawer of my stove)—to recover it.

Ferrets, by and large, enjoy and cultivate their reputation of being found guilty until proven innocent. It's part of their charm.

Thirty-two

The church I'd attended and loved for over a decade had ceased to inspire me, and I made the difficult decision to walk away. After several months of finding excuses not to go to church at all, I woke up one Sunday morning with enough energy and spiritual hunger to search out other places of worship. I visited one non-denominational church, but wasn't too excited over it—only about forty people in the congregation, none of the traditional music that I love, and no greeting from the pastor after the service. But I enjoyed the adult Sunday school class, despite there being only four or five people in attendance, AND I discovered four mini horses in a pen adjacent to the parking lot!

I returned to that church a few weeks later with the expectation of staying only for Sunday school. And I brought with me a container of cut-up apples for *les petits chevaux*. No surprise there. More cars in the parking lot than the first time I'd been there. I walked over to the horses to feed them and love them, and then headed into the church building for Sunday school. Several people filled the classroom, and I received a warm welcome—not just a few curious stares.

When the class ended, I turned left toward the doors exiting out to the parking lot, but that inner voice with which I'm so familiar advised me to remain for the service. Sigh of resignation. Oh, alright. There looked to be close to a hundred folks in the sanctuary this time. I learned later that most of the congregation had been on retreat earlier in the month, which accounted for the skimpy gathering of prayerful souls the last time I attended.

Same contemporary music. Excellent sermon. Lord's Table.

I caught up with the pastor's wife, Cher, after the service and asked if the horses were affiliated with the church. Yes, and mini-horse camp for children during the summer. And, yes, they could use a volunteer all year round to help clean the stalls, groom the horses, and lead them out to graze. At last! A ministry in which I was interested and in which I could participate! AND, Cher informed me, a writers' support group met every Saturday morning in the church building where other authors got together to share and discuss their current work.

I returned to church the following Sunday and met some more people, including Pastor Pete. In response to my request that we meet and talk about the core beliefs of the church, he responded with an enthusiastic, "Yes. Let's do it." He then gave me his cell number and invited me to text him. I did so, and we scheduled an informal meeting at the Chester Starbucks for later that week.

So over hot chocolate and marshmallows, Pastor Pete and I exchanged our stories. I found him to be engaging and open about his faith and his personal history. And I realized that his beliefs and those of the church coincided with my own.

A trifecta of positives: horses, writing, similar beliefs. While not an official member of the church family yet, I believed in my heart that Grace Bible Chapel would become my new church home.

Thirty-three

After an orientation session with Meagan, Cher's daughter, on the care of the mini horses, I began spending every Saturday morning at the barn—at least every Saturday morning that I wasn't away pet sitting.

My first solo with the minis began with the sound of sweet welcoming nickers when I opened the barn doors. Sweetness deteriorated in a hurry as, with full bellies after I'd fed them their breakfast, the little devils played me for the five-foot-short human novice I was at juggling four ponies between two stalls. To whatever ends they envisioned—which had to include driving me off the rails—they choreographed their movements to perfection in such a way that no sooner did I get one of them where I wanted than the others shifted, causing me to chase them. Praise the Lord I'd remembered to close the barn door! No square-dance caller could've had me reelin' and rockin' more so than that quartet of equine whackadoodles.

The "fun" began right after I'd retrieved Queenie's and Earl's empty feed bowls from their stall. No sooner had I turned from fetching Studley's and Duke's bowls than I saw Earl standing in the middle of the barn looking quite pleased with himself. Wait a minute! I remembered being told last week that I needn't worry about locking the chain to each stall every time I walked in and out. "The horses won't go anywhere."

A glance at the closed barn doors subdued imminent panic. I cajoled Earl back into his stall and locked the door. All remained calm for about two beats. And then the circus came to Chester for real when I attempted to herd the horses outside. After tossing two flakes of hay into the corral, I unlatched and entered Earl and Queenie's stall, and opened the door to the adjoining corral. In a perfect world, the two beasties would have walked out and begun eating the hay I'd tossed out so I could then open Duke and Studley's stall, funnel them across the barn, through the second stall, and outside to join Earl and Queenie.

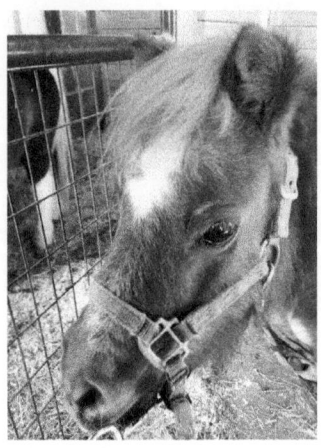

Earl

But that morning in our imperfect world, Earl and Queenie, once outside, feigned interest in the hay long enough for me to open Duke and Studley's stall door, at which time Queenie re-entered her stall, stood at the open stall door to the center of the barn, and barred Duke and Studley from passing through to the outside.

Queenie and Earl

And the stage was set for madcap comedy. Two horses outside their stall, a third one as good as outside her stall—and one human greenhorn laughing to herself in disbelief. You've heard that expression, "How high do you want me to jump?" *Ha!* I could almost hear the chortling horsey speak, "Jump! Higher! Higher!"

So, while praying the wind wouldn't blow the closed but unlatched main barn doors open, I managed to get Queenie back outside, only to have her return as soon as I left the stall to round up Studley and Duke. This scenario replayed three times before it occurred to me to close the connecting stall door to the corral before Queenie could come inside a fourth time. Seemed like a workable plan…until I collected Duke, who became frustrated when he entered Queenie and Earl's stall only to face the closed door. Each time I tried to open it, he either backed out of the stall or moved to the other end of the stall where he stood with his head facing the wall and his hindquarters toward me. "Jump! Higher! Higher!" After countless repetitions, Duke tired of the game and walked outside with just the tiniest bit of arrogant head toss. A hard-charging-from-the-other-side-of-the-barn Studley followed. Guess his herd instinct kicked in. *Phew!* I had succeeded in feeding the four mischief-makers and turning them outside, but the jury continued to deliberate over whether the horses or I had carried the day.

Studley

With the horses fed and corralled, I mucked the much-needed-to-be-mucked stalls, and prepared to leave for home. And as I walked through the barn doors toward my car, something caught the corner of my eye that I hadn't noticed earlier. I turned to look and saw little halters for leading little horses—four of them—hanging on the wall! *Geez!*

Thirty-four

One Saturday morning, while mucking Studley and Duke's stall, and enjoying a state of contented euphoria that only another horse lover could appreciate when engaged in such activity, the world tilted—sideways. Euphoria shuddered, morphed into confusion, and descended into a queer mixture of nervous amusement and mild horror as I stared dumbstruck at the floor from where I'd just pitched a forkful of dirty bedding into the nearby wheelbarrow. How does a seven-inch-long, four-inch-high, picked-clean human or nonhuman bone land on the floor in the middle of a secured stall overnight? With no holes in the wood under which a creature could crawl, let alone one large enough to accommodate a bone the size of a deflated football, I pictured a musclebound raccoon dragging it up and over the stall door and then chowing down in tight quarters while in the company of two mini horses. Ludicrous scenario at best. I left the bone "evidence" on a table in the barn when I'd finished my work. And I wondered…

Later in the day when I mentioned the bone to Cher and Linda, the two primary caretakers of the horses, I drew wide-eyed responses and shrugs from both. Linda had cleaned the stall the evening before, and she had seen no such bone. Maybe, I thought, while continuing to grasp for a realistic explanation, it had been buried in the packed shavings? Pretty thin logic there. Even had that been the case, the size of the bone would have made it close to impossible for Linda to have missed seeing as she raked fresh shavings over the floor.

My need to solve the mystery got the better of me. I messaged Linda Saturday night asking if she would retrieve the enigmatic bone from the barn and bring it with her to church the next day so I could take it to a veterinarian or doctor for identification. I rubbed my hands together in glee as the embryonic skeleton of a "spooky" story began to take shape in my mind.

But any idea of spookiness vaporized after I showed the bone to my vet who identified it without hesitation as part of a shoulder—and not that of a human shoulder. Probably that of a large dog, or maybe a coyote. So much for having found the leftovers of Jimmy Hoffa in a barn on church grounds!

But the question of how the bone got into the stall nagged at my brain. A dark and resolute unwillingness to attribute anything short of a bloodcurdling atrocity to the bone's origin occupied my mind. I no longer searched for a rational explanation, which would be anticlimactic in the scheme of things—the equivalent of Professor Plum doing it in the dining room with the rope. *Pffft!* Hideous circumstances continue to simmer in my imagination, and it may happen that one day I shall feel moved to digress from my stories of nonfiction animal stories, and write my own grisly account of how the bone came to rest on the floor of a locked stall.

Thirty-five

I'd shown up at the barn as usual one Saturday morning and met up with Cher, who thinking I wouldn't be there that day, had already fed the horses and turned them out. Not difficult to understand how she had been confused by my being at the barn one week and not there the next with my summer pet-sitting schedule.

Cher told me when I'd gotten out of my car that she hadn't cleaned the stalls yet or brushed the minis. Brushed the minis? Was Cher encouraging me to groom the horses? What fun! I cleaned the stalls in excited anticipation of hands-on love with the horses, something I'd always enjoyed when I owned Flame.

After I'd finished mucking the stalls, I grabbed Studley's halter from its hook, and his bucket of brushes, and walked outside to the corral. Studley stopped eating his hay and trotted over to me as soon as he saw me with his massage paraphernalia. While I groomed Studley, Dukie approached and stood in line waiting his turn. I finished with Studley and removed his halter, and he stood there for a minute or two as if to say, "Are you finished already?" I returned to the stall for Duke's halter and brushes, and he, too, soaked up the massage,

A quartet of minis

dropping his head under the soft brush when I applied it to his face. Happy couple of littles.

Earl and Queenie's take on grooming differed from that of Studley and Dukie in a big way. My comfort level with the minis had grown, and we'd established the beginning stages of a mutually trusting relationship. But the minis were still the minis, and Earl and Queenie chose to scratch what I think must be their genetic itch for hijinks.

When they saw me emerge from the barn with Earl's halter, they began to move in circles around me along the fence bordering the corral. Studley and Duke watched this development with amusement for about two ticks, decided to go all in, and joined ranks with Earl and Queenie. So now, four horses walked, then trotted, then accelerated into a gallop around me and, in doing so, reenacted the equine formation from the *Ben Hur* chariot race. I couldn't have lunged them in more perfect circles had they been on a lead rope. Thank goodness for a small enclosure!

As they grew more excited or agitated, they wheeled and changed direction as one. Earl seemed to know I wanted to cut him from the herd and stayed on the outside closest to the rail. Studley, the smallest horse and in high spirits, periodically bucked as the horses continued to circle me. And I laughed out loud in spite of myself at their antics.

A momentary break in the ranks allowed me to move in and separate Earl from his partners in crime. I held my arms out at shoulder height behind him and guided him into his stall where he calmed down within seconds and allowed me to put his halter on him. I led him outside, tied him to the fence, and began to brush him. Docile as a lamb, even after I'd finished and removed his halter. He, as had Studley and Duke, then stood beside me as if he wanted me to continue.

I returned Earl's paraphernalia to the barn and reentered the corral with Queenie's halter and brush bucket. Same scenario as when I'd attempted to round up Earl. The horses began to circle, this time with Queenie on the outside. As the minis galloped around me, I tried to think Roy Rogers and his lasso into existence. It took longer for me to maneuver Queenie into her stall than it had for me to "capture" Earl. Even inside, she was skittish, unlike Earl who had relaxed right away—or maybe had resigned himself to the fact that he was done. I talked to Queenie in soothing tones as I walked up to her from behind, and gently pat her rump and sides while she stood facing a corner of the stall. When I approached her head, she didn't resist her halter as I thought she might. I led her outside where she stood while I brushed her. Queenie seemed to enjoy being brushed as much as the boys had, but she insisted on moving her butt around me and away from me when I attempted to brush her hindquarters. I wonder how funny I must have looked scooching around after her.

When they saw I'd finished with Queenie, Studley and Duke approached me with the unmistakable demeanor of hoping for Grooming Session Part Two. I could've stayed in the corral with the horses and loved them for hours. But a meeting at Starbucks with Pastor Pete for the second half of my "Encounter" session, which was required before I could be accepted as a member of Grace Bible Chapel, took precedence. I looked forward to that meeting almost as much as I had looked forward to being with the minis.

Thirty-six

Little things, startling things, silly things, all when mushed up in my imagination and search for wonder, make for interesting times on Schooley's Mountain when I care for Bear, Willow, and Mouse. Take, for example, the series of disconnected events that occurred over three consecutive evenings during one particular assignment with the trio.

While I watched television in the living room the first evening, I heard a kind of muted thump from upstairs. I heard the patter of many feet overhead and chalked the noise up to one or both cats hurtling around as they chased each other, or maybe their own shadows. Bear was not a suspect; he lay on the floor watching television with me. All became clear later when I went upstairs to go to sleep, and saw that the shower rod had slipped and fallen onto the floor. Maybe Willow or Mouse had pulled it down in their exuberance. Not outside the realm of possibility. I slid the rod back into place as best I could, although not quite as straight and not as high as it had been. It's that vertically-challenged thing again.

Loud and bright thunderstorms the following night, which I may have slept through had Bear, the German Shepherd-Collie mix, not been frightened enough to jump onto the bed, curl up almost in my face, and begin to shake with anxiety. Poor thing! I staggered downstairs for his anti-thunder apparel and tranquilizers. His tranquilizers—I couldn't find them anywhere, so Bear went cold turkey with only his thunder shirt and my arm wrapped around him until we both fell asleep.

When I awoke next morning, Bear was still on the bed. Most unusual. His normal procedure is to sprawl somewhere on the bed after I've just gotten under the covers with a book—and sometimes before I've gotten under the covers. Those nights when I'm not fast enough to jump into bed before him, Bear leaves me with a scant foot of space after he's stretched out over half the mattress and all the pillows. His facial expression, devoid of malice, reflects no guilt from his commandeering of available sleeping area. But during the night, every night, he vacates the bed maybe to do a sweep of the house, and returns to sleep on the floor either beside the bed or in the bedroom doorway where he protects me from gargoyles come to life, and assorted other non-thunder-induced monsters.

Bear

And why would the third and last night of the assignment prove any different from the previous two nights in its provision of smiles? Vinny and I had paid a fare-thee-well visit to The Chatterbox, a legendary and much-loved-by-motorcycle-and-car-enthusiasts hamburger joint that would be closing its doors in a few months. A bittersweet occasion as we listened one last time to the disk jockey spinning 45s from the fifties and sixties on his turntable, and enjoyed a final burger and black-and-white ice cream soda at the one-of-a-kind Chatterbox. When we returned to Bear's house, Vinny walked me to the front door, kissed me good night, and then headed home. I walked past the darkened living room with only the hall light for illumination, and saw the easy chair in the corner slowly rocking. Enough supernatural experiences have found their way into my life that most don't phase me anymore, but a chair rocking by itself gave me a start. A skipped heartbeat and a quick blink or two, and I saw the heavy drape from the open window behind the chair blowing in the breeze with enough force to rock the chair ever so slightly. Shook my head, chuckled a relieved chuckle that no poltergeist shared the house with me, and continued up to bed.

Awesomeness, sometimes sad awesomeness, happens during daylight also on the mountain. How can it not when untamed nature around the house teems with wildlife? Early one morning, I looked out across the lawn and saw what appeared to be a rabbit missing its ears hopping across the far end of the wooded backyard. Later in the day, I saw the "rabbit" come to feed on the sunflower seeds I'd tossed out for the wild things. The critter turned out to be a squirrel that had had a large part of its tail severed—and not too long ago judging from the rawness of the injury. I tore myself away from the sliding glass doors through which I watched various small woodland denizens chow down their breakfast, but not before the image of the mutilated squirrel had burned itself indelibly into my mind. How I wish I could have captured the animal and taken it to a vet! Even though the sight of him caused my stomach to heave, I kept a lookout for "Stumpy," as Robyn and her family had named him to see how the absence of a tail affected his ability to be a squirrel. I felt comforted and happy to see him make tracks across the ground, climb a tree, and balance on a branch as well as any of his kin.

Of the many perks that come with these assignments, a favorite is the opportunity to feed a small herd of deer that visits every evening around dinnertime. One doe, Sally, had been coming for a couple of years, and was semi-tame. She would stand just off the back stoop and wait for me to toss saltines to her from where I sat on the steps.

Then during one assignment, I saw she'd injured one of her legs. But she limped up to within about three feet of me. I may have been able to tempt her even closer, but I didn't want to encourage her to step onto the area of large gravel that separated the lawn from where I sat. The single biggest problem I had with feeding the deer was finding the heart to stop throwing food to them. I once tossed half a sleeve of saltines to Sally, after which she stood there and asked for more. Her babies, which she'd brought with her one season weren't interested in saltines, and stayed on the far side of the yard.

Mouse, the once-outdoor cat before being rescued, continues to hear the "call of the wild," and eyes the glass door in anticipation of making a break for it every time I open it. Robyn tells me they let her out on occasion, and she always comes back after a short time. But I prefer to keep her indoors. I have containment so far.

GREEN ACRES

One morning while walking with Bear, he insisted on escorting me over a new hiking path that I'd never seen. Kudos to the man who funded what I discovered to be a beautiful trail through the lush woods just across the street from where Bear and his family live. As we walked it together for the first time, Bear led me through what I sensed were magical woods, like something out of a Tolkien story. The ambience permeating the trees called up a profound silence that bordered on surreal. No birds twittered. No squirrels ran their apparent haphazard routes up one tree and down another. No chipmunks scooted before us only to give us the slip among some nearby rocks. I could almost feel the eyes of reclusive enchanted wolves, snakes, and owls upon us as we made our way deeper into and among the trees and ferns. But Bear, with his arthritic hips, seemed to be on a mission and strained forward at his leash, unwilling to cave—even after having navigated several ascents and descents of the path. Only after serious discussion and the promise of a second woods adventure the next day did he agree to turn with me for home.

Bear and I share an excellent relationship. The following day when I delivered on my promise to him, I trusted him off-leash once we'd walked down the first steep hill, maybe a hundred yards into the woods. I watched with joy as twelve-year-old Bear appeared to recapture his youth as he loped ahead of me. And as I knew he would, he always waited for me to catch up before putting too much distance between himself and me. In fact, the only time he "disappeared" was when the perfect place to poop happened to be about fifty feet or so off the path. A moment of panic on my part when I lost sight of him, but to watch him come running back, jumping and clearing a small bush…Good boy!

We walked deeper into the woods than we had the first day as Bear showed no sign of tiring, and I enjoyed seeing him so happy. Our extended hike took us past some cantaloupe-orange-colored mushrooms, the likes of which I'd never before seen. Thought they'd have made a most excellent perch for the stoned caterpillar that Gracie Slick immortalized in the sixties rock anthem, "White Rabbit."

Bear and Willow

Another twenty minutes or so of walking through, and breathing in the magic of those woods. Then, a sense of non-magical reality: As far as Bear and I hiked, we had to retrace that distance to return home. *Sigh.* So I reached down deep—deeper than my inner child for whom the concept of common sense didn't exist—and made the adult decision to turn around and head back. Bear hesitated for about a second before running up alongside me and retaking the lead. The return walk seemed much shorter than the walk into the woods had been, and my inner child pouted and made the legitimate case for maybe sometimes listening to her. I sat down on the large rock where I'd originally released Bear so that he would come back to me, and allow me to releash him for our approach to the street. The pedometer on my phone claimed Bear and I had traveled more than two miles—up and down hills, over some rocks. Not bad for a couple of young-in-spirit old bodies.

Thirty-seven

Three hours spent texting and emailing two clients in an attempt to massage the month of August into nonconflicting assignments for both parties obliterated any chance of my developing a "this is too easy" attitude about the behind-the-scenes work of pet sitting.

The initial email arrived sometime in February at 9:30 in the morning. Robyn (Bear's mom) in Long Valley wanted to know my availability for one week the following August, one of two consecutive weeks that I had already penciled in for Debbie (Buddy and Keno's mom) in Montville. A series of emails ensued involving the firmness of Debbie's plans, and the flexibility of Robyn's plans. The back-and-forth session wrapped up at 12:30. End result: Robyn and Debbie retreated to their respective corners to think about what they wanted to do while the pet sitter sat in a pathetic heap and thought, not for the first time, that she needed to look into hiring some help. The situation resolved itself a couple of days later when Rob, Robyn's husband, changed his vacation from the third to the second week in August. I would leave their house and drive straight to Montville at assignment's end.

Debbie and Robyn had bumped into each other the previous August as well, except that that time after I'd left Long Valley, I retrieved Buddy and Keno from where they'd already been boarded for one week, and returned with them to their house for one more week. As described in my earlier book, this visit turned out to be the one in which Buddy and Keno were "off their food" for a short time.

And a few years prior, Robyn and Ann (Sassy's human) needed a sitter for the same time. Robyn had reserved me months in advance for one week in August so she and her family could visit Chincoteague, Virginia. Ann called sometime later requesting two weeks in August so she could attend her family reunion in Tahoe. Because the second week was the same week I'd committed to Robyn, I called Robyn to check that their plans were firm. If so, I would of course give Robyn priority.

Robyn, however, didn't want me to lose out on a longer assignment, and after talking it over with Rob, they postponed their own trip by one week. I was floored by Rob's and Robyn's generosity and willingness to accommodate me (and Ann). Rescheduling their plans had to have spawned complications, especially with three young children. But Rob and Robyn epitomize most of my client pool: loving, generous, and possessing humble hearts that put others before themselves. For my part, I reduced my fee for them and prayed that Mother Nature would favor the family with perfect weather. As I recall, she did.

"And we know that in all things God works for the good of those who love him, who have been called according to his purpose." Romans 8:28 (NIV)

Thirty-eight

After grieving the loss of their beloved Jada who had made her way to Rainbow Bridge a few years earlier, Susan's and David's hearts healed enough to rescue another dog. And beginning on Good Friday, a month after they'd brought her home, I had Laika, a three-year-old Rhodesian Ridgeback mix in my care for nine days.

Circumstances unfolded from the first day of the assignment that filled me with a kind of dread about the current adventure in which I'd enrolled myself. A note left on the kitchen table advised that I would have no television except for DVDs. And because I hadn't brought any of my own... *Uh-oh!* Thank goodness for the entire Harry Potter series, which I'd seen several times but still enjoyed, in Susan and David's collection! Note to self: Update packing list to include DVDs.

And during my initial few hours with Laika—the time during which I'd intended to acquaint myself with the dog—I found myself in a situation of having to stare down the devil. Susan, unaware of my complete and incurable helplessness when faced with chocolate, had left a bag of the confounded stuff on the kitchen counter. A Gollum-esque argument between my two selves ensued within my head:

Good Stormie: Susan and David didn't know.

Bad Stormie: There's so much; they won't miss it if you take a few pieces.

Good Stormie: It isn't even opened!

Bad Stormie: *Scoff!*

Good Stormie: Walk away!

Bad Stormie: From Lindt Lindor's Dark Chocolate?

Good Stormie: It might be for Easter!

Bad Stormie: From Hershey's miniatures?

Good Stormie: Hide it!

Bad Stormie: Hide Ghirardelli Intense Dark Chocolate?

Good Stormie: Yes! Hide it and forget about it!

Bad Stormie: Idiot!

And as Bad Stormie slunk away to whatever dark recesses of my being she inhabits, Good Stormie buried the chocolate high in the pantry behind a couple of boxes for safekeeping. Who knew I possessed such fortitude? Not me.

With the seductive chocolate out of sight, I resumed my bonding with Laika, a sweetheart who turned out to be a strong, and stronger-willed dog. Her partially collapsed trachea dictates that she can tolerate no pressure on her throat, so she wears a harness only, which puts her handler at a severe disadvantage when it comes to the issue of control.

And her attention span when on-leash likened itself to that of a ferret. Oh! That shiny thing over there! That smell over here! That drumming sound from behind me! And what's that thing—that fuzzy thing—moving over there across the street? Laika felt compelled to investigate every smell, every sight, every sound…and I, a simple human who could compete with none of the outside stimuli, ceased to exist in her mind during our outings.

LAIKA OUT OF CONTROL

As a result of Laika's insatiable curiosity and well-developed shoulder muscles, our first few walks together were nightmares, battles of wills between the out-of-control dog and helpless-to-gain-control me. She lacked any apparent desire to please unless it suited her. She refused to focus on me. She ignored my voice when I attempted to call her to me after she'd tugged the leash to its max. When I stood in front of her, she moved her head to look around me or through my legs, or worse, turned her entire body to face another direction. A smack on her rump resulted in the brief look of annoyance she might bestow upon a fly that brushed against her. And her obvious knowledge that I could do little or nothing to modify her behavior without a collar around her neck convinced me I would be in for a rough nine days.

Laika

Her clear defiance frustrated me to no end as I recalled the words a professional dog trainer had once said to me about the absolute necessity of gaining and maintaining a dog's attention when leashed—for its own safety, that of others, and my own. I researched (and I hate research!) approved training techniques, and took to draping Jada's old cotton loop leash loosely around her neck and carrying treats in my pocket when Laika and I walked. I stopped in my tracks the instant she began to "get strong," and called her back to me. Getting her to return to me continued to be a problem that would try the patience of a saint. But it took only two separate times of my adjusting the loop high behind her ears and just behind her jaw bone (away from her throat) to prevent her from lowering her head and throwing her weight against the harness—kind of the opposite principle of a martingale bridle used to keep horses from throwing their heads back in resistance to the bit—for her to realize that attempting to remove my left upper arm from its socket was no longer a good idea. After that, it became a simple matter of getting her to respond to me without hesitation, to sit before me, to receive a treat, and to remain sitting until I released her. I continued to walk her with the loop draped loosely over her neck and shoulders as a reminder to her (in case she decided to test me) that I would win every future struggle, either the easy way or the hard way.

PROGRESS / SMALL VICTORIES

Early morning walks with Laika proved to be the most challenging. I had to be mindful of the difference between her urgency to do her business after eight or nine hours in her crate, and her desire to tug at the leash for the sake of tugging at the leash.

But there were moments when she made me so proud of her. Like the time, she saw a squirrel a ways up the street, and every wound-to-maximum-tension spring in her body released. *Boing!* Earlier in the week, she'd have been all over the map and out of control, but that morning, I reined her in without application of the loop behind her ears and got her attention with relative ease, asked her to sit, gave her a treat, and asked her to "Wait!" Once seated, she remained so on a slack leash, albeit quivering like a leaf in a stiff breeze, until I said, "Okay, let's go." Granted, the squirrel gave Laika lots of time to absorb and process my repeated command to "Wait" as it strolled with unnerving calm across the street—so unlike the typical helter-skelter ricocheting gait of its kin.

And then there was the night she scared up a skunk when we returned from her late-night potty break. Or rather the skunk, indifferent to our presence, walked across the lawn maybe fifteen feet in front of us minding its own business when Laika, who'd been SO great on the leash most of the day (lulling me into a false sense of achievement with her), lunged and nearly ripped the loosely-held leash from my hand. "Laika!" and a swift smack with the leash across her shoulders brought her back to me in an instant and had her sitting before me and focusing on me instead of the skunk. "Good girl! Wait." After I'd given her a treat, Laika continued to sit and wait. And the skunk, a laid-back critter, continued on its way across the moonlit lawn, groovin' to whatever vibes that skunks groove to when feeling happy and unthreatened. Visions of uglier endings to the evening leapt into my head, and I thanked the universe for this one happy skunk.

I discovered that when within the confines of the house, "within the confines of the house" being the operative words, Laika learned commands in record time. She had "drop it" down cold in two days. She understood "sit" and "wait" within a day and a half, and interpreted "wait" to mean "Stop whatever it is I'm doing. Sit. Focus on Stormie until she releases me, even if I'm standing at a wide-open door to the outside." She proved her ability to learn and internalize commands when asked to wait in the connecting doorway from the mudroom to the deck while I adjusted the gate at the entrance of said deck. And she waited until I said, "Okay!" before stepping outside. Smart dog!

PLAYTIME

Laika's favorite interactive pastime with humans involves roughhousing, although her loud menacing growl while playing tug o' war gave me pause the first time I heard it. Given that she's part pit bull, the sound of her deep-throated snarl reminded me to check and evaluate the rest of her body language before I continued the game. Once I'd determined that she was all about play, and she realized she'd found a willing playmate in me, a high time was had by both of us.

I learned firsthand one morning that Laika's pit-bull jaws have the strength of a steel trap. While playing an "all-in" game of chase and tug, my hand got a tad too close to her mouth. Not Laika's fault, and no broken skin, but the force with which her teeth closed for a split second on my thumb! Tsunami-like waves of pain washed over me to the point that I thought I would pass out. And I wondered if she'd damaged a nerve when the tip of my finger went numb for a couple of minutes.

Laika, meanwhile, oblivious to my concern over a possible injury inflicted by her, continued to head butt me in the thigh with the little rubber pig with which we'd been playing as if to say, "C'mon! C'mon! C'mon! It's the fourth quarter! You can't wimp out now!" So I finished the quarter with her in what amounted to ten minutes, and then trusted her home alone and outside her crate for an hour and a half while I went to the gym and took on the comparatively easy challenge of pressing dumbbells. When I returned home, Laika waited at the back door to greet me, and all blankets and other forbidden-for-Laika-to-chew artifacts were intact. *Yes!!*

Laika is one of the few dogs I know who has little tolerance for the time I spend working on my laptop. The stubbornness she exhibits when on-leash takes the form of pushy insistence on getting my attention when she thinks I've ignored her longer than she deems proper. To that end, she'll bring her ball-on-a-rope or some other toy to me and porpoise-bump me—hard—in the knee or thigh until I either acquiesce to her demands, convince her that I don't want to play (doesn't happen too often), or open the door onto the deck to let her outside.

HITTING THE DECK

The deck! Laika loves hanging out on the deck where she can watch all the goings on in the neighborhood. She patrols the deck without a sound until another dog or a cat enters her line of sight, and then bark, bark, bark. But one sharp knuckle rap from me on the glass in the door leading from the mud room to the deck, or on the sliding glass doors off the kitchen startles her into silence. When she isn't on high alert for creatures on the ground below trespassing on or too close to her territory, she chases the bumblebees that busy themselves zigzagging overhead. I watched her run back and forth attempting to catch them in her mouth, and thought to myself "sooner or later, Laika…"

During the time I stayed with her, Laika chose to remain outside all day, every day (unless it was raining)—coming in only for meals, a game of tug or chase, or some cuddles. The hours she spent out of doors benefited her on multiple levels: physical conditioning as she performed her laps and ascertained she missed nothing, mental health as different stimuli acted upon her brain, and psychological well-being as her contentment and calm clearly evidenced. All things necessary to the happiness of a young dog. I look forward to when Susan and David fence in their backyard so Laika has more room to run.

Early on in my visit with Laika, several vertical slats loosened and dislodged from the deck's gate leading to the street, which left a gap through which Laika could fit, and which prevented me from leaving Laika outside without supervision. A day or two later when bright sunshine warmed temps into the upper seventies, I took it upon myself to repair, if only with a temporary fix, the hole in the gate. The basement contained all sorts of odds and ends, as does any basement, so I began my search there and in short order found a large piece of crosshatching that might have been from the side of an animal's crate. I also located a fair-sized metal box filled with sand. Excellent! The steel grate just covered the opening in the gate, and the heavy sand-filled box along with a couple of large flower pots from the deck, anchored the grate in place and allowed Laika access to the deck without my having to be outside with her.

When the time came to say goodbye to Laika, I felt the usual mix of emotions when ending an assignment: I would miss her, but I looked forward to returning home and getting back to my-time-is-my-own lifestyle. I couldn't help thinking that Laika epitomized a textbook example of a dog that with diligent training and an exercise regimen appropriate for her age, size, and breed, could develop into a perfect family pet. Laika needs only to internalize the concept of "my human is my Alpha dog" to be a calm and, by extension, happy dog.

AFTERMATH

Four days after I'd concluded my time with Laika, I went to the gym, got a pedicure, and later that afternoon, became almost paralyzed by pain as every muscle in my upper left quadrant—intercostal, trapezoid, pectorals, shoulder—screamed upon the slightest movement. It hurt to bend. It hurt to reach down. It hurt to reach out or up. It hurt to breathe. And being that my left side is my dominant side, I was pretty much knocked out of commission. A cocktail of a muscle relaxant and Tylenol 3 failed to provide relief. A follow-up hot shower felt good but did nothing to alleviate the pain. In desperation, I went to the ER where I received a shot of some uber pain killer in my shoulder, and what amounted to an "I don't know what's causing the pain" diagnosis from the doctor. I took comfort in at least hearing that the EKG and Xrays revealed no heart problem, no bone cancer, no bone fractures, and no dislocations.

Despite the injection of the designer drug I received in the ER, the pain level had not subsided by the next morning. I still couldn't sit up, bend over, reach for something without help, and without wincing in pain. The best I could manage was to keep my arm stabilized against the side of my body, and sweat with anxiety and pain.

A visit to my orthopedic surgeon and a second set of Xrays revealed an inflamed (not torn) rotator cuff, and the absence of arthritis and all other "itis-es." Following a cortisone shot in the shoulder, orders to take two Advil every eight hours, and receipt of a special exercise regimen, I bade farewell to the orthopedic people in hopes that all pain would go away within a month.

And I remembered my week with Laika and my near-constant effort to keep her on my left side. Damaged rotator cuff—occupational hazard?

Thirty-nine

Fourteen days after I concluded my assignment with Laika, I was slated to be with Warren—a charge I thought I'd lost as Mary and her husband hoped to buy a house in North Carolina where John is stationed. I looked forward to my time in Dover with the rescued Bichon who was always an easy assignment, something for which I was grateful, especially as I recovered from my rotator cuff inflammation.

And then an unexpected wrinkle: Mary texted me less than a week after my injury to tell me that Warren had developed a compressed vertebra that resulted in a marked limp. Two weeks of a Prednisone regimen had had little effect, and he still favored his right shoulder and front leg. Because he was not supposed to be jumping onto and off of furniture or climbing stairs, Mary had been carrying the fifteen-pound Warren up and down the two flights to her apartment, and sometimes for part of his shortened walks if he appeared to struggle taking steps. Mary, having no idea of my own injury, asked if I would be okay with extending his care to accommodate his injury.

As it happened, I felt close to one hundred percent by the time Mary notified me of Warren's situation. I'd continued with Advil as needed, and exercised at the gym every other day for the past week. I thanked God that I'd had ten days to recover, and felt comfortable with the prospect of picking up and carrying Warren as necessary.

Animals "listen" to their bodies more than we humans do. Of this, I'm certain. As if realizing that he wasn't in peak condition, Warren peed as soon as I took him outside, and then continued to his favorite spot in which to poop half a block away without stopping to mark every vertical object as was his norm. When he'd finished his business, he turned around and headed home. He kept up a good pace as he hobbled, but I missed our walks through the center of town with him strutting like the biggest and baddest dog around.

Warren made no attempt to jump up on the furniture. Rather, if I were on the sofa, he'd gimp over to me and utter soft, almost apologetic whines until I picked him up and put him on the sofa with me where he'd sleep for as long as I remained there. Or on occasion, he might inch over to within a foot of where I sat and beg for attention to his poor damaged little body by sitting and posing stock still with a lifted right paw in a pitiful but award-worthy display of dramatics. His mournful facial expression while waiting for me to heed his plea for attention—priceless, and almost always impossible for me to resist.

In an effort to find some relief for Warren before leaving him with me, Mary had taken him to an acupuncturist, and hired a massage therapist to work on him in the apartment. Warren responded well, albeit for a short time, to both treatments. And Mary had scheduled two additional massages for him while I was with him, which thrilled me to pieces. I couldn't wait to see the proper technique employed in massaging a dog.

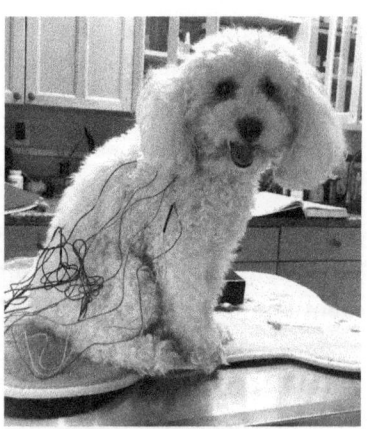

Warren with accupuncture

When Dawn arrived for the first massage session and sat on the living room floor with Warren, I watched in awe as he relaxed and smiled while she imbued his hurting body with healing positive energy. I soaked in as much information as Dawn volunteered, and absorbed all sorts of tidbits on the dos and don'ts of massaging dogs or any other animal. "You have to wait for the animal to let you in." "You can't force your way into muscles and expect to do any good." "The animal must trust you before it will relax."

While disappointed that Warren didn't trust her quite enough to lie down during the session, Dawn didn't push him. Instead, she took whatever Warren would give her. She told me that he was a lot better than he'd been the first time she'd seen him when he wouldn't let her touch his sore leg. When the session ended, Warren surprised both of us—maybe even himself—by jumping up on the sofa under his own power.

Dawn must have known her stuff during those sixty minutes. Pre-session, Warren had hobbled about like a geriatric wracked with old war injuries. Post-session, he felt so much better that while on our afternoon walk, he stepped out like he owned the street. And when we returned home, he barreled up the two flights of stairs at a near gallop rather than waiting for me to pick him up and carry him. Then he waited for me on the landing, grinning big. "Look what I can do!"

The morning after his massage, he scared me by not stirring when I got out of bed and said good morning to him. I walked over to him and looked closely to make certain he was breathing. Yes, slowly and deeply. I massaged his ears, and Warren opened heavy-lidded eyes, picked his head up, and leaned into my hand with a luxurious stretch and yawn.

And when we embarked upon our early morning walk in the third straight day of rain, he trotted out with his limping much less defined than twenty-four hours earlier. Maybe another benefit of Dawn's therapy included a night of pain-free sleep for Warren.

Later that day, Warren snuggled up to me on the sofa for a scritch, and I attempted to appease him with a reasonable replication of Dawn's technique. While I'm sure that whatever healing energies I may have transferred to him in twenty minutes fell far short of those from Dawn's fingers, I believe Warren appreciated my efforts. He kissed my face and fell asleep on my lap.

Warren was a trooper, bless his heart, and with the exception of his what I'd come to believe were justified dramatics, he did his best not to complain about the discomfort he endured, even maintaining a zippy pace when walking. When we returned from our walks, he always looked like he was smiling with his mouth open and tongue hanging out, but I think his panting may have been from exhaustion and/or pain, even though we traveled only halfway down the street or until he pooped, whichever came first.

While massages were much appreciated by the little guy and afforded him short-term relief, I believe they could do little to eliminate the physical cause of his problem. And I wondered if he made things worse for the rest of his body by favoring his right front side—much as when a human favors an injured body part—throwing his spine and everything else out of whack. I noticed he turned his right foot out when he stood (not good for spinal alignment), and it seemed to take him longer to find a comfortable position in which to lie down.

As time passed since his therapy session, Warren's pain level increased. But he continued to follow me around the apartment, and I got into the habit of trying to organize myself in such a way that I minimized my walking back and forth to make it easier on him. I looked forward to the next appointment with Dawn, which was scheduled for the last day of my assignment, three days after his last session. Since Warren's comfort level improved so much after one massage...

The second therapy session did not disappoint. Warren's trust in Dawn increased to the point that he lay down while she worked on him, and he even bestowed a few kisses upon her face. When we took him for his post-massage walk, he made it clear that he wanted to walk farther than just halfway down the street. And since I always let him tell me where and how far he wanted to walk, around the block we went for the first time since I'd been there. Not to discount the benefit of Dawn's treatment, but I never underestimate the therapeutic value of dry weather on aches and pains. And after three consecutive days of rain, I was finally able to trade my rain hat and gum shoes for sunglasses and sneakers.

An update from Mary a few weeks after she'd returned home informed me that neck-focused chiropractic and acupuncture treatments had had little effect on Warren's condition, although the compressed vertebra showed signs of improvement. The vet thought it time to shift chiropractic focus to Warren's shoulder, and Mary has begun to see progress in Warren's condition. "His adjustments seem to be holding better now."

But because Warren had favored his right front leg, holding it off the ground as often and for as long as possible, the muscles in that leg had atrophied, and one of the leg's tendons had shortened and tightened to the point where he could no longer place his paw flat to the ground without stretching—kind of walked on tiptoe with that paw. Mary began leading him in physical therapy twice a day, and massaging his leg with an essential oil called New Mobility.

At last update, Warren has begun to put more pressure on his foot with less obvious pain, and is walking greater distances with less of a limp. Acupuncture and chiropractic treatments continue every other week, and future massage therapy sessions with Dawn are planned for maintenance, along with lots of prayers for Warren's full recovery.

Forty

Flash, a twenty-year old black cat, was thin and frail but otherwise healthy when I cared for him. His brother, Gordon, a long-haired white cat whom I never got to know other than to feed, change his litter box, and wither beneath his unblinking stony stares, had made his way to Rainbow Bridge a few years earlier.

I enjoyed my assignments with Flash. His house, situated high above the road and surrounded by several acres of woods, provided a retreat-like experience for me—one in which my biorhythms dropped, my mind cleared, and my productivity at the computer increased.

Until the last year of his life, Flash could make the leap from the floor to the kitchen counter where he'd watch the birds at the feeder outside the window. He wasn't allowed on the counter and I never caught him in the act, but his paw prints on the black granite always gave him away.

Flash devised a unique way of alerting me when it was time to change his litter box. Despite his age, he would hurtle around the house, back and forth along the length of the hallway, up and down the stairs, for no apparent reason. I came to learn he'd engage in this behavior after having a good poop. Pretty much like any living crea-

Flash

ture, even if we humans don't celebrate with Flash's enthusiasm!

Flash's vast repertoire of meows cracked me up. For instance, if I were working at the computer when he felt it was time for me to feed him (which was almost always), an assertive meow pulled my attention from my typing to the little cat that had crept up behind me and stared up at me with accusing eyes. And if I didn't jump right away, a second meow followed in tone and volume that could only mean "Now!" Those times when I refused to be intimidated by Flash's demands, he skulked away not to be seen or heard from again for maybe half an hour when he'd return and insist that he would keel over from starvation if not fed this instant. It seemed an insignificant matter to him that he ate four times a day: breakfast, mid-morning snack, mid-afternoon nosh, and dinner.

Other times, he'd emit long plaintive yowls for no discernible reason other than to remind me that he continued to suffer from malnourishment, and that it would behoove me to feed him before he became psychotic from hunger. He'd walk down the hall with slow plodding steps toward the den where I read or maybe watched television, and I could hear his dismal wails growing louder as he approached. His cries made the mournful strains of "Ghost Riders in the Sky" sound like a sweet lullaby.

NOW YOU SEE IT

Gordon

A picture-perfect September afternoon when I arrived for the beginning of an assignment with Flash. I checked under the welcome mat where Sue always left the key for me. But I didn't see it this time under either mat. *Hmm.* A quick circuit of the large Victorian-style house revealed nothing except windows too high for me to reach, and locked doors. I checked as many potential hiding places as I could find (under rocks, in and under planters) for a spare key. I looked in the garage, behind and under all the typical garage stuff, as well as in the console of the one car remaining in the garage. Went so far as to call the church Sue and I attended in hopes that Harry our pastor, or anyone he knew in the church might have a key to the house. Harry knew of no one who could gain access into the house but, full of fun as always, suggested I try a brick through the window. I rechecked under the mats…well, because I've had experience with things being not in a certain place the first time I searched, only to have them appear in those same places the second or third times I searched. Not this time.

    I peeked through the large glass windows in the walnut entrance doors as if by seeing the foyer, I could will myself inside. Or maybe I thought I could summon someone from a parallel universe to unlock the door. Flash, the only body, spectral or otherwise inside the house, sat in the hallway and watched me with a concerned look on his face. Time for his afternoon nosh drew nigh.

    Having run out of options for gaining entrance into the house, I left phone messages describing my predicament for Sue and Don who were at that moment jetting to California. I had no idea when they would land, so I parked myself on the front porch steps and spent the time daydreaming in the wooded setting and considering how many worse places I could be stuck.

    Less than an hour passed before Sue returned my several calls, each sounding more desperate than the one before. She insisted that she had put the key under the mat. "But it isn't there!" Okay. Sue would call Don's parents (Don and Marilyn) whom she thought had a key to the house. In response to Sue's SOS phone call, Marilyn drove the half-hour from their condo to where I sat on the porch feeling both relieved and embarrassed when I saw her car pull into the driveway.

I'd met Don's parents a few years earlier when Don had encouraged them and me to hunker down at their house during the massive power outage resulting from superstorm Sandy. Marilyn was a fireball, sharp as a tack, with an easy sense of humor. This day, as she disembarked from her car, she laughed at my predicament and inserted her key into the door of the house. But it didn't turn. Marilyn admitted it was an old key, and the lock may have been changed since the key was last used. But we tried every lock in every door we could find before Marilyn realized it was a key to the house that Sue and Don had lived in before buying this one.

Maybe Don's dad had a newer key. "C'mon. Let's get down off this mountain where there might be better cell service…and a bathroom." Ten minutes later, in the parking lot of a Long Valley strip mall, Marilyn phoned Don's dad. The call went to voicemail.

Marilyn continued to laugh at the situation, and said it provided the perfect opportunity to visit with each other and spend some girl time together. I was happy to let her enthusiasm rub off on me.

We next thought to find a locksmith in the yellow pages, but no hard-copy yellow pages in existence since the explosion of cell phones onto the scene. *Sigh.* And no locksmiths that we found online answered their phones. *Double sigh.* Instead, we accepted with gratitude a hard copy list of local locksmiths from an optometrist in the mall, and after studying it, settled on one that looked nearby and didn't have an 800 number. But before calling the locksmith, Don called from Lake Tahoe, and insisted the key had been left under the mat the night before.

In continued good spirits, we returned to the house where Marilyn again attempted to contact her husband to see if he had another key, one that might fit the door. And I for the heck of it returned to the porch and again looked under the mat. *Are you kidding me?* The key lay there plain as day attached to a long one-inch-wide pink-and-green-striped strap! How could I have missed it the first time? Or the second? I held it up to show Marilyn who dissolved into gales of laughter at the sight of it.

I walked over to her car and gave her a hug with sincere and mortified apologies. Marilyn, however, thought it was all great fun. I could see her laughing still as she drove back down the driveway and headed for home.

Not like things of this ilk hadn't happened to me before. As I let myself into the house to reassure Flash with a plate of delicious kibble, I remembered a time when Steve and I had wanted to take our motorcycles for a spin. But neither of us could find my helmet. We searched the entire house several times over. The helmet was nowhere to be found. And then on maybe the third or fourth lap, I again went into the bedroom and saw the helmet—a big blue full-face thing—sitting on our bed! Steve and I had checked the bedroom multiple times and had not seen it. So along with that itty bitty but insistent voice that guides me around life's curve balls when I heed it, a mischievous force now and then wreaks havoc by causing objects to disappear and reappear in space and time. Frustrating, but part and parcel of my life and the lives of others who share mine.

Forty-one

Soon after I'd returned home from my assignment with Flash, Vinny removed our bedroom air conditioning unit from the window for winter, something we don't bother to do anymore. While I cleaned the kitchen after breakfast, Vinny came up the stairs carrying a large folded towel much like a cushion on which a page might carry his king's crown. But no crown rested on the towel that Vinny presented to me with something akin to pride. "Look what I found." I looked at him from across the room and saw some kind of a dark still creature against the blue towel. Thinking it was something that had been killed, my stomach lurched. "Take it away. I don't want to see it."

Vinny turned to head back down the stairs with his prize when curiosity got the better of me. "Wait. What is it?" "A bat—a live bat. Found it holed up inside the air conditioner." I moved in for a better look, having never seen a bat up close, and I saw the cutest little brown animal. Vinny held the bat gently on its back in the soft towel. Poor critter had to have been terrified. Or maybe it was just angry, because it kept opening wide its mouth and revealing its big teeth. Way big teeth for a small animal!

We took the bat outside and attached him to the side of a large oak tree from where we hoped he'd find a comfortable and sheltered place to hang upside down and sleep the day away before embarking on his evening foraging for a meal of mosquitos and beetles.

The bat

Forty-two

A short autumn assignment on Schooley's Mountain with Bear, Mouse, and Willow, and I'd been just about to lead Bear out through the garage for his 6:00 bathroom break when I heard something crackle—like an opened bag of potato chips that won't stay closed after you've folded the top down. Heard it and dismissed it. Bear's garage contains all kinds of stuff (a fleet of bicycles, outdoor maintenance paraphernalia, containers of cat litter, an assortment of bags and boxes...) that if bumped or nudged by the wind (of which there was plenty that night in advance of an approaching storm) could squeak, hiss, or rustle in protest.

After Bear finished doing what he had to do and we reentered the garage, I heard again that same out-of-the-ordinary crinkle beside the steps leading up to the door to the interior of the house. This time, I turned and sought the source of the sound. My imagination? Or did that large bag of sunflower seeds at the bottom of the steps ripple? I moved in for a closer look. Jiggled the top of the bag. A disproportionate crackle in response. Momentary hesitation, and I jiggled it again. Same response. But this time, the bag moved with relish, continuing to do so independent of my poking at it. And it dawned on me that something—some *living* thing—was holed up inside that heavy plastic bag.

My first thought, and I remember it well, was of a bear concealed in the forty-pound bag of sunflower seeds! I continued to stare at the bag, which had lapsed into silence and adopted the stationary stance of any well-behaved inanimate bag. Some small degree of common sense prevailed and banished thoughts of tiny sunflower-pilfering bears.

But a modicum of sound judgment was no match for my need to know what was inside that bag. I reached over and poked the bag. Much agitated rustling. Couldn't leave well enough alone, could I? With no appearance of evil-looking fangs or claws poking over the top of the bag, and with no hint of nightmarish hisses or growls, curiosity got the better of me. I crept over to the bag for a peek inside. Oh, to have had my cell with me! My temporary nemesis, the would-be bear, turned out to be a startled ravenous chipmunk!

Forty-three

I'd never accepted an assignment over New Years until Joyce, a good friend of mine who'd been there numerous times for me in the past when I'd required help, needed a sitter for her eight-year-old ginger cat, Tuffy, whom she'd adopted a few months earlier.

Tuffy met me at the door when I arrived. But when he realized I wasn't Joyce, he removed himself to a vantage point on the floor between the kitchen chairs from where he could keep a more-curious-than-hostile eye on me, and form some kind of objective opinion of this not-Joyce human.

Despite Tuffy's initial mild rejection of me, I sensed a profound calm permeating Joyce's warm and simple condo.

As I'd expected, all things—and I mean ALL things—panda surrounded me. Hundreds, no, thousands of panda likenesses jockeyed amicably for position among the knickknacks, blankets, kitchen utensils. If a panda image could be imprinted onto or into an object, said object existed in Joyce's home. Christian keepsakes balanced out the riot of pandas without being heavy-handedly religious. End result: a cheerful, uncluttered, everything-in-its-place setting in which I would spend the next seven days decompressing from real life outside of panda-dom and breathing deep easy breaths. With Tuffy and Feliza (a fantail betta fish) for company, I anticipated a productive week with little, if any, interference between my muse and me. But, as it happened, communion with my muse would have to wait…

The universe applauded my peace, and chose to deepen my sense of well-being by indulging my not-so-inner pluviophile with a torrential storm. I, in anticipation of Mother Nature's performance, bolted upstairs to the bedroom where I lay supine on the bed as clouds thickened and lowered. I allowed myself to enter a Zen-like consciousness as the first raindrops splashed onto the skylight. And while the clouds emptied themselves of lifegiving rain, I glanced to my right at the nightstand and saw what I hadn't noticed earlier when I unpacked.

Tuffy

Joyce had created a "Welcome" station for me, complete with earplugs in case I forgot to bring mine, a mask (panda motif, of course) in case I forgot to bring mine, and a neat little book of short stories about cats. And best of all, she'd put together little cellophane-wrapped and ribbon-tied bundles, each containing two Hershey kisses and a scripture verse—one packet for each day I'd be there. A five-star hotel couldn't have made me feel more comfortable or cozy. And as the storm ran its course, my soul leapt with those "Let's go!" vibes associated with re-energization. Time to write!

I'd gotten busy at my makeshift workstation on the kitchen table when I heard a scratching noise and the banging of the bungeed-shut doors to the under-the-sink chemicals behind me. I turned in my seat just in time to see Tuffy, who knows he isn't allowed on the counter, standing on his hind legs—like on kitty tippy toes—reaching as high as he could with his front paws, and pulling the dish towel and a saucer on which I'd placed his second serving of treats to the floor. A clap of my hands, and a sharp "No!" prevented him from gobbling up more than a couple of the scattered treats.

I wondered if Tuffy's mischief was him acting out because he was mad at me for having made him work so hard doing tricks earlier for his first helping of treats. He couldn't know or understand that Joyce liked to make him "think" when she gave him his treats and had, in fact, encouraged me to do the same during my meet and greet with him a week earlier. One of the games she sometimes planned for him involved scattering the treats in a large box filled with crinkled brown wrapping paper. Sounded like a good idea to me, so I'd followed suit. It was fun to watch and listen to him paw through the paper in search of the treats. Tuffy may or may not have been amused.

Fish care unsettles me almost as much as plant care, and Feliza did little to assuage my uneasiness by appearing sluggish, languishing at the bottom of her bowl, not even swimming to the surface to gobble food when I fed her that first evening. More disconcerting, she showed no interest in the food that floated down past her when all she had to do was open her mouth and inhale the flakes. Last time I'd seen her, when I first met Tuffy, she was swimming around like a happy fish. I wondered if she could be missing Joyce.

But as I lay in bed later that night, I remembered that Feliza is a tropical fish, and who knows? Maybe she was cold. I'd lowered the thermostat to sixty-nine degrees when I arrived. Could that four-degree drop in temperature have affected the water and made her uncomfortable? I jumped out of bed, went downstairs, and upped the thermostat to seventy-one. She seemed better the next morning, occupying herself with picking in the gravel for bits of food and otherwise engaging in what looked like normal happy fish behavior.

We had two Black Mollies during one hot summer when I was growing up. Our second-floor apartment had no air conditioning, and the window fan did nothing more than blow hot humid air into the living room. My mother, not knowing any better, put ice cubes into the fish bowl to cool the fish. Because the internet didn't exist back then, she couldn't research the care of Mollies and learn that they require water temperature between seventy- and seventy-nine degrees Fahrenheit. Her misguided good intentions resulted in the expected sad outcome.

I have to chalk up my New Year's Day episode of "Stormie's-Believe-It-Or-Not Stupidity" to too much partying at a friend's house, and not enough sleep the previous night. After feeding Tuffy (and Feliza) and cleaning his litter boxes, I began my personal care morning ritual. Well, I *attempted* to begin my ritual, but knocked my toothbrush off the shelf and into the freshly cleaned litter box on the floor below. So I carried the brush downstairs to the kitchen and sterilized it in boiling water, after which I returned upstairs and brushed my teeth.

Had anyone told me that a day would come when I would clean my teeth with a toothbrush that had fallen into a litter box, fresh litter or not, sterilized or not, I'd have thought they were crazy. But it was New Year's Day, and I had committed to staying in my jammies for twenty-four hours and watching football. A trip to the local pharmacy for a new toothbrush was not an option.

Wanting to avoid having to retrieve my toothbrush from cat litter a second time, I thought to stand it up inside the spare roll of toilet paper on the shelf rather than laying it on the shelf where I could knock it off again. A reasonable idea, right? Well, because there wasn't enough clearance between the shelf and cabinet above it for me to stick the brush into the roll, I removed the roll from the shelf and dropped the toothbrush into the tube—the tube that's open at both ends! And the now-wet brush took a second plunge into the litter box! I can't make this stuff up! *Mercy!*

Joyce texted me after she'd seen my post on Facebook, and encouraged me to take one of her unopened toothbrushes.

I watched *The Godfather* on television the third night I spent under Tuffy's care. And despite him cuddling with me on the sofa offering all the feline calm he could, after two-and-a-half-hours of graphic violence, I was struck by the incongruency of the movie and the general ambience of my panda-filled sanctuary. The pervasive peace of Joyce's condo cringed in patent revulsion.

Emergencies happen. I love my clients. I love "my" animals. And my personal and professional desire is to minimize for everyone as much stress as possible brought on by unforeseen crises meted out by a capricious universe. To that end, I assure all clients that should circumstances develop that impede their return home (delayed/canceled flights, traffic, inclement weather, etc.), I will stay with their pet(s) as long as necessary—hours or days—within my ability to do so, or return to their house if I've already left.

Sometime during the late morning of my last day with Tuffy after I'd returned the condo to the condition it was in when I first arrived (put fresh linens on the bed, vacuumed the carpet, emptied the dishwasher), and packed my bags, I received a phone call from Joyce.

"What's your availability to stay with Tuffy a little longer?"

"Of course! Define 'a little longer.'" (I had another assignment slated to begin a few days from then.)

"Not sure at this time, but will call you later."

Joyce, it turned out, was in a Maryland hospital emergency room on her way home from Williamsburg, and in enough pain to think she had a kidney stone. Her parents who had celebrated New Year's Eve with Joyce were still in Virginia, but would meet Joyce at the hospital.

At 3:00, I received a text from Joyce saying she was being admitted to the hospital, but would get back to me with plans/options after speaking with a second doctor. No problem. I could think of less pleasant places than Joyce's condo to remain for an extended visit.

"Longer" turned into a twenty-four-hour extension with Tuffy. And in case I'd ever doubted the perks of my job, the audible relief and appreciation in Joyce's voice when I promised that she need not worry about her kitty's care filled me with a warmth equaled only by Tuffy's phenomenal cuddles. Such a blessing!

DRIVING MR. TUFFY

Some months later, Joyce received and accepted an offer to assist in a neighborhood ministry in Kentucky—a big move from New Jersey, and what seemed like a perfect fit for her abilities and passions.

But the illustrious and mighty Tuffster doesn't like car rides. Hates them. Associates them with going to the V-E-T. In an attempt to desensitize Tuffy to his fears before the three-day journey south, Joyce asked if I would be willing to sit with him in the back seat of her car and speak soothing words to him while she drove around for maybe forty minutes—longer than he'd ever been in a car. Sure, but I get car sick. How's about I drive, and she sit in the backseat with Tuffy and encourage him? Agreed.

Tuffy

So while Joyce engaged in a running monologue of soft-spoken Tuffy affirmations, I concentrated on driving Joyce's Cobalt that has neither a clutch nor a six-cylinder engine like my Xterra. Perhaps because it required no manual shifting, the little car increased its speed with little effort or realization on my part. Had to apply the brakes several times after seeing the speedometer register that I was rocketing along at ten or more miles per hour faster than the posted speed limits.

~ Stormie's Heart ~

Between eavesdropping on Joyce's murmurs to Tuffy, keeping the little car within safe-from-ticket-producing speeds, and trying to make for an as-feline-therapeutic ride as possible, I failed to see the cop car's flashing lights behind me until a whoop from its siren startled me into consciousness. Knee-jerk reaction: pulled over immediately. But unused to the light weight of Joyce's car and its tight turning radius, I cut the wheel too sharply to the right and felt the car heave almost as if the left tires had lifted from the ground. And for good measure and added thrill, I almost hit the curb and saw a couple of tree trunks up close—really close. Always cognizant of the impression I make upon others (*giggle*), I had the presence of mind to glance around to ascertain no one except the cop (who continued wherever he was headed without even acknowledging my stunt-driving antics) had seen my less-than-stellar reflex action. Joyce, bless her heart, remained calm throughout the pulled-from-an-old-time-cartoon-chase clip. Prevented me from getting crazy, too.

Tuffy, my "anxiety-ridden patient," fared less well. He had been so good for the twenty-five minutes we'd been on the road. But after my near miss with all sorts of looming immovable objects, he pooped in his crate. Poor baby. We turned into a nearby parking lot where Joyce cleaned Tuffy and his crate with her ready supply of Tuffy- and crate-cleaning supplies. I opened the window for some much-needed fresh air, and as we headed toward home, the frightened Tuffy peed… and pooped again. A forgiving kitty, he accepted my apology in the form of scritches behind his ears when he'd been released from the crate after returning to his condo. I hope he feels it was all worthwhile when he gets to his new digs in Kentucky, and sees the large bay window that overlooks fields and trees, and his own room with windows on three sides so he can follow the sun all day long.

Forty-four

I saw what I recognized as a sharp-shinned hawk in our backyard depicting in stark relief the beauty and savagery of nature. The large blue-gray bird picked at some small critter that I couldn't identify (thank you, God!) at the edge of our woods. But I'd served up walnuts to a company of squirrels half an hour earlier, and a sense of nagging guilt over having lured a squirrel to its death haunted me for the remainder of the day.

Later that spring, I saw a large Cooper hawk (identified from a photo online) perched on a low-hung branch only feet from where a couple of terrified squirrels crouched frozen in place, either on other branches or on the ground near the embankment in our backyard. The memory of losing a fuzzy creature to a hawk not long ago propelled me from the kitchen to the dining room in a hurry where I opened the window as fast and with as much noise as I could. "No! Not again! Thou shalt not eat my critters! Go!" And wonder of wonders! The bird, having shown every inclination of partaking in a live buffet, turned its head toward me in annoyance, thought better of grabbing a quick meal, and took flight. A beautiful bird indeed. But I

~ Stormie's Heart ~

don't want to see the circle of life enacted in my backyard. I feel queasy enough watching robins pull worms from the dirt!

Forty-five

An assignment of firsts. The first for a family member. The first out of state in Pennsylvania. The first that involved the care of chickens, in addition to five indoor cats and two outdoor feral cats.

Had it not been Vinny's niece who needed a sitter for her animals, I'd have declined the two-day assignment at the outset because of the half-hour trek on Interstate 80 to her house. Turned out the drive at 6:30 on Saturday morning of the Labor Day weekend wasn't too terrible, and the fabulous view of the Delaware Water Gap from Adrienne's backyard negated what little anxiety I'd experienced en route to her house.

As soon as I arrived at the house, the immediate need to pee took precedence over unpacking my truck or enjoying the view. Jumped from my car, tapped in the garage door combination, ran through the garage to the connecting door to the house…and found it locked. Ran back to the car. Lifted the hatch while beginning to twitch, fished out my laptop bag, and retrieved Adrienne's file and house key from the compartment in which I'd stored them. Back across the garage to the door. When I unlocked the doorknob and still couldn't open the door, I realized the deadbolt needed to be unlocked as well. By good fortune, the same key fit both locks. But when I opened the door, I found myself not in the house, but outside on the deck. With my bladder ready to burst, I ran across the deck to the door opening onto a hallway off her kitchen. And then a bit of déjà vu. Locked. I unlocked the doorknob with the same key I'd used to enter onto the deck, and when that door wouldn't open, I realized that yet another deadbolt also needed to be unlocked. Through the second door into the foyer where I saw a bathroom located just inside the door. And not a moment too soon!

Elsa

A pretty Siamese-mix cat greeted me with a kind of purr/hiss/growl—more interesting than frightening—and accompanied me into the bathroom where I enjoyed a moment of profound relief.

Four-year-old Elsa began life living on the street where an untreated bacterial infection developed into chronic rhinosinusitis, the cause of her wheezing. In the near-complete silence of Adrienne's house, a solitude I hadn't experienced since I'd lived in my Chester cottage fifteen years ago, Elsa's raspy breathing spooked me a couple of times during my stay in Pennsylvania.

Ian, another sweetie, was blind in one eye as a result of some trauma when Adrienne found him homeless on the street. After being neutered, Ian made it clear he wanted no part of being released back "into the wild." So Adrienne adopted him as a permanent member of her "family," and had his injured eye surgically removed. These days, Ian receives liquid phenobarbital on his food for seizures, and liquid pilocarpine to treat obstructive constipation.

Nic, a reclusive ginger, tracked me from the shadows during my first full day at the house. By the second day, he felt comfortable enough to feign polite interest in the U.S. Tennis Open for a bit while sitting a short distance away from where I plopped on the sofa. A real leap of faith for Nic, and I wished I didn't have to leave the next day. Maybe we could have become friends.

Adrienne found Sonic (II), the prettiest of black-and-white tuxedo kittens, in a local shelter. Kismet! Having lost her previous black and white (also named Sonic) two years earlier, the tuxedo in the shelter cage seemed to Adrienne like Sonic reincarnated. The current Sonic, and the youngest of Adrienne's menagerie at four months old, ran from me always except at meal time.

Ian

Feeding times required a magician's dexterity and a saint's patience. As soon as they sensed I was about to prepare their meals, Sonic and Ian arrived in the kitchen, leapt onto the kitchen counter, and pushed their noses into the bowls before I filled them. I mixed Ian's food and medication first, and then guarded the bowl with my arm, shoulder, head—whatever it took—from Sonic who made every attempt to steal Ian's food. When I finished preparing both bowls, I fed the two cats, one at each end of the counter, and then grabbed the other bowls and the appropriate feed for the remaining three cats, Elsa, Nic, and Augusta (a Maine coon, who hid in Adrienne's bedroom closet almost all day, sometimes with Nic). Elsa could almost always be found downstairs. Speed was of the essence here because Sonic, upon seeing me run off to feed the others, would leave his own unfinished meal, launch himself from the counter, and chase after me. And that little cat moved like greased lightning.

Mealtime choreography occurred twice a day. After the third or fourth performance, I developed a standard operating procedure which worked most times: feed Ian and Sonic, feed the cat(s) in the master bedroom closet before Sonic could catch me, close the bedroom door, feed Elsa downstairs after closing the basement door.

Once barricaded downstairs, I could then scoop corn from the bin in the "chicken room," and feed the waiting small herd of deer that arrived in the backyard like clockwork when I fed the other animals. Loved seeing the stragglers lope across neighbors' lawns toward me when they saw me carrying the bucket of corn, and walking out to where I would spread their feed.

And then it was time for the chickens. The chickens! A trip in and of themselves. Thank goodness there were only three—two hens and a rooster.

On clear mornings, the first trick (after pulling disposable booties over my shoes to protect them against the inevitable stepping in copious deposits of chicken poop) involved capturing the birds, one at a time, and carrying them outside from their basement quarters to their outdoor playground—a large fenced-in area and coop. The large brown hen, Marcie, was easy to catch. Kate, the black and gold Mohawk, not so easy, but once cornered, didn't put up much of a fight. And Pippa, the Rooster, led me a merry chase around the room before realizing that if he wanted to go outside with the ladies, he must allow me to carry him. All the chickens, once cradled in my arms with their wings secured, became docile when being transported. And all appeared happy when reunited, clucking to each other, and pecking at their feeder, which I filled and took out for them each morning.

The final step on the list of morning chicken care: clean their indoor room. For this segment, I added thick elbow-length rubber gloves to my ensemble for scraping up as much chicken mess as I could and dumping it into a plastic bag. The one fun thing about this task was locating fresh eggs, either inside the coop or in the bedding on one of the tables in the room. Finding my first egg left me almost as ecstatic as when I discovered a Ghirardelli dark chocolate peppermint bark bar in Adrienne's cupboard.

Clean four litter boxes, and the indoor morning chores were almost done. Time to take my shower, pick up any feed bowls that I'd brought downstairs, and head upstairs to open the basement door where Elsa almost always waited on one side to be released to the rest of the house, and Sonic and Ian waited on the other side to race downstairs. Open the bedroom door and remove Nic's and Augusta's feed bowls.

After I'd showered and shined, only two animals remained to be fed: the outside cats. A simple procedure. Both waited on the deck for me each morning and evening, but the tortoise-colored cat hightailed it away as soon as I opened the door. The ginger, though wary, held his ground. As a result, he usually got the dollop of moist cat food on top of both bowls of kibble. Adrienne told me he allows her to get close to him and pet him, and sometime soon, she plans to have him neutered and placed in a forever home. Maybe had I been there another week or two, I could have gotten on petting terms with him as well.

While at Adrienne's house, I opted for the downstairs bedroom as opposed to one of the two on the main floor—a decision that appeared to disturb the cats. All five of them, even the antisocial Augusta, crept into the bedroom the first night, sat on the floor at various stations around the bed, and fixed me with enigmatic stares as I settled in to read as I always do before falling asleep. But not one of them joined me on the bed. And since no cats remained in the bedroom the next morning, I can only guess they'd wandered off to embark on whatever nighttime activities they'd planned after realizing I was harmless and not all that interesting anyway.

When I'd finished reading for the night and turned out the overhead light, pitch blackness engulfed me. Perfect! Even the LED display on the nightstand clock wasn't lit. And since I'd unplugged all the nightlights downstairs when I first arrived, the depth of obsidian darkness was complete. No need to wear my sleep mask in that house!

But I needed to walk several feet through the main room in the basement—the room where kitty toys littered the floor and simulated a veritable minefield of booby traps into which I could step—to the bathroom. Good thing I had thought to pack my miner's light, which Vinny had given me one Christmas. Kept it within arm's reach on the nightstand.

I also employed my earplugs in case Elsa returned to the bedroom. Didn't want to be jolted awake by the sound of a nearby night creature's snorting and hissing.

Compliments of the wide, for the most part unbroken vista from Adrienne's kitchen window, I caught two spectacular sunrises—not just the awesome horizon-to-horizon striating swaths of color ranging from pale gold to deep purple that backlit the mountains, but the distant fog, too, that collected and hung between the dark tree-covered ridges like the breath of a reclining giant. As if God Himself stretched an energizing stretch, sighed a luxurious sigh, spread His arms wide with joy in His Creation, and bestowed life-giving light and beauty onto the world.

I'd noticed upon my arrival at the house an exquisite red maple tree having the same color leaves and accessible low branches as the copper beech I used to climb on my grandmother's property. A wave of nostalgia warmed me. For a brief moment, I entertained ideas of climbing Adrienne's tree, too—just for old time's sake.

The red maple pulled at my viscera with relentless persistence until I could resist it no longer. So a few hours after sunrise on the second morning, I surrendered my questionable adultness to the indulgence of my inner child. Tree time—if only onto the first branch!

Shedding my crocs inside the house, I trotted across the front yard to the tree. Wanted to feel the grass and dirt beneath my feet, and absorb the energy of the earth as I made my way to the tree. And I wanted to feel the bark under my feet. But said bare feet hindered me from climbing higher than the first branch. Or maybe a potent sense of caution or fear that seeped through my entire being as I sought for purchase on even the lowest branch with my toes—a feeling that I don't remember experiencing when I was ten and climbing trees—may have played a part in inhibiting my scramble up the tree. I resigned myself to the fact that my days of pretending to be a squirrel monkey in the forest had passed.

Much to my delight, several hummingbirds visited the two feeders Adrienne had hung outside her living room window. I wanted in the worst way to get a video of those birds, to the point that I even missed a couple of games of tennis waiting for just one hummingbird to cooperate. Every time a bird came to drink and I moved to align my cell phone in the slightest, my would-be subject flew away, warned off his friends, and I wouldn't see another bird for several minutes. After half an hour of snatching glances at tennis while I spent most of the time looking out the window, attempting to perfect the Zen-like art of moving without moving, I decided to crouch and wait a few feet from the window with the phone at the ready. My knees cramped and my fingers shook as I held the phone with the camera zoomed on the feeder waiting for another hummingbird to visit. Driven by my refusal to be out-waited by a bird the size of a walnut, my efforts were eventually rewarded with a short but decent video.

The stillness at Adrienne's retreat, broken only by the occasional cock-a-doodle-doo from Pippa in the backyard or a choked hiss from Elsa, lent a comforting sense of remoteness to the house. And the weekend passed in peace between tennis and laptop time and cat visitations.

But those chickens! They needed to be brought back inside at dusk. So the first evening I was there, I walked across the lawn to collect them. Marcie, again, wasn't too difficult to catch, and I carried her back to the "chicken room."

Walked back to the pen to retrieve Kate where she and Pippa had worked out some kind of tag team thing that had me at a severe disadvantage from the get-go, and gave me fits. Outmaneuvered with ease by a pair of chickens! I finally corralled and captured Kate, much to

Pippa's dismay, and carried her back to rejoin Marcie in their nighttime barracks.

And then steeling myself for a second go with the pesky rooster, I headed back to the pen where I discovered Pippa's stubbornness rivaled that of my own Wookiee. Despite missing Kate and expressing all sorts of anxiety in chicken speak, he refused to let me catch him and carry him inside to her. So round and round the coop I chased him in the pen. Several times, I backtracked thinking I could catch him as he rounded a corner of the coop almost into my arms, but he'd squawk, flap his wings, and reverse direction before I could get a hold of him. And because I didn't want to hurt him by making a wild grab at him… But thoughts of shooting the bird dead leapt unbidden and unhampered into my mind more than once. And to further confound my efforts to retrieve the cursed Pippa, a freshly laid brown egg rested on the floor of the pen (because I'd forgotten to open the door to the coop when I'd taken the chickens outside that morning). When Pippa flew up to the roof of the coop, I thought I had him. But right before I could clasp my two hands around him, he half-flew, half-scuttled onto the ground, and I was left standing there, glaring at him, and wishing again for a shotgun.

Then I remembered Adrienne saying that Pippa would follow Kate anywhere, including across the lawn and back inside. Taking Adrienne at her word, more out of desperation than anything else, I opened the pen. Pippa ran out and across the yard. But instead of going to the back door of the house as I'd expected and hoped, he flew up onto the deck railing from where he cut a handsome figure indeed. The beginnings of panic roiled my stomach juices. And then he began to crow! Bonehead! It's dusk! Get your internal clock straight! I gave thanks for tolerant neighbors, or maybe neighbors who laughed behind slightly parted curtains for the last half-hour as they watched three scheming chickens and one simple human mix it up. Pippa came to ground after a minute or two. But every time I opened the door to let him in, both hens were at my feet looking to make a dash for it to freedom. *Oh, great!*

I closed the door, left Pippa outside to his own devices, and put Marcie and Kate inside the coop after yet another game of chase with Kate. When I opened the door to the yard. I saw that Pippa had returned to the deck, and was again in full voice. *Resigned sigh.* I left the door to the chicken room open and backed away in hopes that Pippa would indeed want to rejoin his lady love. He did. I closed the door behind him, released the hens, and considered taking Adrienne up on her offer to help myself to anything I wanted behind the well-stocked bar.

Second day playing chicken woman. By mid-morning, the day had turned chilly and damp, and dark clouds approached from the east. Decided to bring the chickens inside, even though I'd turned them out only a couple of hours earlier. Better to corral them ahead of time, rather than have to chase them around in the rain, and maybe thunder and lightning.

Again, I returned Marcie to the chicken room with little effort, and prepared for the traditional game of chase around the coop with Kate and Pippa. After a couple of laps, I noticed the door to the pen was ajar, and when I bent to pull it shut, Kate flew up and landed on my back between my shoulder blades. My surprise at having a chicken roost on me was nothing compared to Pippa's agitation as Kate settled in for the long haul. While I marveled at her strategy for capture prevention, I wondered how long my body could sustain a chicken-supporting posture.

And then Pippa, who had been circling me on the ground and fretting about Kate's abandonment of him, also flew up to the Stormie perch. But he launched a frontal assault and landed on my head. My instinctive reaction to duck and cover resulted in Pippa clawing through my freshly washed hair (*Ouch!*) as he sought balance before moving down my neck to my shoulders, where he displaced Kate to my butt.

~ Stormie's Heart ~

This was one for the books! I removed my cell phone from where I'd stashed it in the back pocket of my jeans, and after a short photoshoot, apologized to my hitchhikers and slowly straightened my spine. Gravity exerted its inevitable influence, and Kate, Pippa, and I resumed our laps around the chicken coop. Maybe, I remember thinking, these feathered creatures will grow on me as I spend more time with them, but right then, I couldn't help wondering why anyone whose last name isn't Purdue would choose to keep chickens in the first place.

On the road home by 6:30 Labor Day morning. Five lanes of wide-open highway stretching to the horizon, and classic rock pumping from the speakers of my satellite radio. "Radar Love." "Ob la di Ob la da." A pale memory brightens in my mind: I used to love to drive. Adrenaline rush with the realization that I still love to drive—fast—when no more than twenty cars travel in my direction on Interstate 80 the entire way home from Pennsylvania. "Witchy Woman." Crank it up. I imagine my Xterra low and sleek, and further indulge my reverie by rewinding time to 1984 when my ride was a Mustang GT convertible. My old friend. Still miss her. "Love Me Two Times."

Forty-six

I received an email from my Montville clients in the beginning of June 2019 that set me back on my heels: "We've put our house on the market, and have a potential buyer. If all goes according to plan, we will move to Lavallette (down the Jersey shore, about ninety minutes away) by end of August." *Gleep!* One of my favorite clients—gone! The email continued with the tempting offer of a night in a local-to-their-new-house hotel so we could check out the area. And Debbie would compensate me for gas and time if I agreed to stay on with them as their pet sitter.

Vinny, who loves the beach, was thrilled. But because I'm not crazy about beach traffic or shoulder-to-shoulder people in the sand, he doesn't get down there much. Debbie's proposition sounded like a win/win for Vinny.

In addition, Teri (she with the two Pomeranians) has a sister who lives across from the hotel where Debbie had volunteered to put Vinny and me up if we decided to scope out the situation. According to Teri, the hotel is located less than a quarter-mile from blocks of big beautiful houses on the bay, probably the area to which Debbie would be moving. A lovely town in general.

I weighed the pros and cons of accepting Debbie's offer, and the biggest checkmark in the "cons" column had to do with my fear of driving for extended periods of time on high-speed heavy-traffic-volume roads like the Garden State Parkway. Not sure when I morphed into such a wuss. Maybe it's a consequence of growing older, or the realization that a lot of people tend to do all kinds of things behind the steering wheel beside pay attention to driving.

As one might expect, I have my GPS set to the shortest route rather than the fastest route to get from any Point A to any Point B. And when I plugged in the address of the hotel in Lavallette, it avoided the Garden State Parkway altogether in favor of Route 35. Traffic lights all the way down, except for a short time on Interstate 287, added maybe half an hour to the commute. In my opinion, well worth the time to avoid the anxiety of four lanes of traffic moving at eighty miles per hour or better.

So I talked to Debbie and agreed to try it once with the caveat that I could not commit to being there for their January or February junkets because of my hopeless and undeniable inability to drive in snow. Probably should have added March to my reservations as well, given the way winter has hung on the past couple of years on the east coast.

Buddy

During what I knew would be my last assignment in Montville, it became clear that Buddy had lost most of his sight. He walked with hesitant steps, and required diligent guidance around poles, fire hydrants, sewer grates, and up and down curbs. Keno, on the other hand, suffered from impaired hearing—although I couldn't determine to what degree his disability might be selective. Even when napping, he heard me and woke up when I opened the door to the cupboard where the treats were stashed.

Fred and Gene, the kitties, continued their thyroid medication. But Fred, who had developed some fluid build-up around his heart, now receives Lasix to combat labored breathing, and Atenolol to regulate his heart rate. Time takes its relentless toll on all living things, including animals.

I almost have to shake my head in bemused acceptance that, as with so much of my time spent with animals, those four days (a short visit compared to most Montville assignments) with the Montville crew were not without incident or drama.

Debbie had advised me that a pesticide crew would be spraying the dog park on Sunday morning, so I'd put off taking the dogs for their outing until after 1:00. Both dogs were happy to find an energetic friend in the large-dog enclosure when we arrived. Keno loped around with him, and Buddy played a little "sniff and jump away."

Fred

When the owners left with their dog, another person arrived soon after with two Shih Tzus and went to the small-dog enclosure. Keno engaged in some exuberant barking with one of the little dogs, and attempted to entice him to run the fence with him. Sadly for Keno, the Shih Tzu would not be engaged, and walked away to join his owner after losing interest in whatever it

Gene

was that Keno had to say. Keno, with an air of resignation, followed suit and lay down next to the bench on which I sat.

Meanwhile, Buddy wandered off, using the perimeter fence as a guide. And I watched in horror as his left hind leg appeared to buckle under him. Thinking he'd had some kind of a stroke, I ran over to him as he continued to "walk" while his hindquarters periodically collapsed to the ground. He seemed better after I'd leashed him, called Keno to me, and led the dogs to the car at a snail's pace.

But Buddy would not or could not jump onto the ottoman I placed behind the car. I circled him around, much as one circles a horse back to a jump it at first refuses. After several passes without success, I was at my wit's end as to what to do, and Buddy appeared anxious. A Borzoi is a large dog; think Afghan hound. No way could I lift him up and into the hatch. The man with the Shih Tzus couldn't see what was happening, because my hatch door was raised and blocked his view. I considered walking back to the enclosure and asking for his help, but Keno was already in the hatch and standing on the edge waiting for his cookie. And I couldn't leave Buddy standing there outside the car in the parking lot.

Then an idea! If I could lift Buddy's front paws onto the ottoman, support him from underneath, take as much weight as I could off his hindquarters, and then kind of "walk" him forward on his front legs until he was up against the hatch, only about eight inches higher than the ottoman, he might step inside. Praise the Lord! He did just that! Cookies all around!

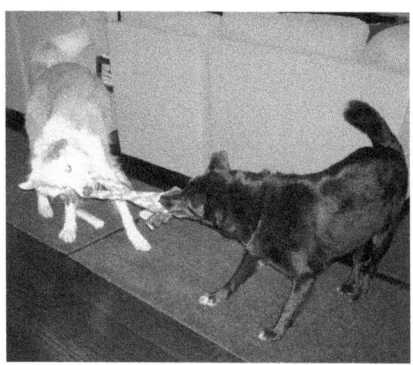

Buddy and Keno in younger days

When we arrived home, Keno jumped out with no encouragement. Buddy, however, was afraid. I spoke to him in soft tones, held him on a short leash, supported him with one arm behind his front legs and the other in front of his hind legs, and semi-lifted him out to the ottoman and then down to the ground after he'd committed to jumping. In retrospect, I think it took a good deal of courage on Buddy's part, not to mention faith and trust in me, to leap out when he couldn't see where he was going. After riding the elevator upstairs, Buddy walked into the foyer, and stretched out in the warmth of sunbeams on the hardwood floor where he slept away the afternoon.

Keno and Buddy in younger days

I watched Buddy like a hawk the remainder of the day and saw no further sign of weakness in his leg, although he did appear to stand with it splayed a bit. But after seeing him launch himself onto and off of the bed, which is almost twice as high as the ottoman and a couple of inches higher than the hatch of my truck, I'm willing to grant (and hope) that any perceived misalignment of Buddy's leg could have been nothing more than my overactive and rattled imagination making more of an anomaly than necessary.

Erring on the side of caution, I didn't take the dogs to the park the following day, but settled instead for an easy second walk later in the afternoon.

And since I never heard anything to the contrary from Debbie, I found comfort in assuming that even the temporary weakness in Buddy's hindquarters was a freak thing, a mere harmless departure from the norm brought about by something as simple as maybe the equivalent of a charley horse.

~ Stormie's Heart ~

I don't know if I'll ever see Buddy, Keno, Fred, and George again now that they've moved to the other end of the state. But if I don't, I thank them for the laughter and memories with which they enriched my life, and I wish them and their humans many years of continued joy.

Lightning Source UK Ltd.
Milton Keynes UK
UKHW042132081020
371260UK00002B/49/J